TOWARD A
MODEL
of
Constitutions

TOWARD A
MODEL
of
Constitutions

WILLIAMS KUTTIKADAN

HOUNDSTOOTH
PRESS

Photos on the Cover

Top row (left to right): Nelson Mandela, Hippocrates, Mencius, William Wilberforce, Kwame Nkrumah, Martin Luther King Jr., and Ferdinand de Saussure.

Middle row: Adam Smith, James Madison, Simon Bolivar, Edmund Burke, B. R. Ambedkar, M. K. Gandhi, and Hannah Arendt.

Bottom row: Eleanor Roosevelt, Ayn Rand, Abraham Lincoln, Florence Nightingale, Isaiah Berlin, Immanuel Kant, and Montesquieu.

All the photos are in the public domain.

Toward a Model of Constitutions

How Human Rights, Lincoln's Address, and Berlin's Liberties Explain Democracies

ISBN 978-1-5445-3039-0 Hardcover
          978-1-5445-3038-3 Paperback
          978-1-5445-3040-6 Ebook

*This book is dedicated to
the democracies of the world and
all those who are striving to
keep them that way*

Author's Note

What if Constitutions can be understood as diagrams? What if crucial concepts like the separation of powers and rule of law naturally emerge in the diagrams, without us trying to include them? This book introduces a visual approach for understanding Constitutional structure—a generalist approach requiring no special training.

For instance, despite this book being about Constitutions, it cannot claim to be a "legal" work, since it does not study the specific laws of any given country. Instead, this work is based on the conceptual understanding of human rights. Indeed, the direct inspiration for this work was Wikipedia's article on Rights.

The fact that the Rights distinctions in that article (covered in the third chapter) stayed unchanged for a decade certainly brought a strong focus to this work. But, given that the resulting learnings have not ceased even after a decade of effort, it is safe to say that many aspects of Constitutional structure remain unexplored. Consequently, this work should be treated merely as a beginning and not an end, which partly explains the title—*Toward a Model of Constitutions*.

Notably, since concepts used in the later chapters are introduced in the earlier chapters (usually via diagrams), the chapters have to be read in sequence. Not surprisingly, stopping to understand all the details may take time and effort. Fortunately, apart from the first and third chapters, most other chapters are a shorter, easier read.

Chapter Outline

Part One
OVERVIEW *of* THE MODEL

1. A Constitutional Structure
2. Separation of Powers and Rule of Law
3. Background Theoretical Considerations
4. Avoidable Misinterpretations

Part Two
PEOPLE'S EXPECTATIONS *from* SOCIETIES

5. People's Expectations from Sovereignty
6. People's Expectations from Democracies
7. People's Expectations from Developed Democracies
8. Avoidable Misinterpretations

Part Three
SHORTCOMINGS *of* THE MODEL

9. Self-Correction and Monetary System
10. Ambiguous Areas in the Model
11. Failure Points in the System
12. Avoidable Misinterpretations

Contents

Part One
OVERVIEW *of* THE MODEL

Part Two
PEOPLE'S EXPECTATIONS *from* SOCIETIES

Part One

OVERVIEW
of
THE MODEL

1

A Constitutional Structure

> *"For to be free is not merely to cast off one's chains,*
> *but to live in a way that respects and*
> *enhances the freedom of others."*
>
> **—NELSON MANDELA**

This work attempts to model a Constitutional structure by approaching it as an exercise for protecting and increasing individual liberty. To achieve that aim, we have to bring together several areas that are usually not dealt with together. These include the likes of logic, ethics, human rights, Constitutions, organizational boards, and protection of private space. But the traditional area most closely related to this work is that of human rights.

The main idea is to develop an analytical framework that can increase the efficacy of existing human rights, while remaining within the paradigm of the Universal Declaration of Human Rights (UDHR) from 1948.[1] To be more specific, the framework attempts to improve human rights in people's public spaces, while staying outside of people's private spaces.[2]

1. CONSTITUTIONAL STRUCTURE

This model's structure is explained in three parts. The first part will identify the starting root element. The second part will look at eight complementary elements that are added sequentially to build up the model.[3] The third part examines the final ninth element, which must be complementary to the whole model that has been built up to that point.

A. Starting Up:
Life/Liberty as the Root Element

In the first part of the model, the root element of the human social system is represented by human life itself. After all, it cannot be subdivided further, nor can it be ignored in anyway as a redundant element. Life

---

[1] United Nations. "Universal Declaration of Human Rights." www.un.org/en/universal-declaration-human-rights/ (Last accessed on May 3, 2022).

[2] The improvement is theoretically possible because the model addresses the structural aspects of the legal space, which is an area that a traditional human rights approach tends not to address. However, the model is incapable of specifying any real details about the people's private spaces because of its logical, structural approach. Therefore, suggestions regarding the private spaces will have to come from UDHR-like norms.

[3] The *complementary elements* approach was conceptualized as a direct result of trying to understand the theoretical distinctions present in rights theory: Claim–Liberty Rights, Negative–Positive Rights, Individual–Group Rights, and Natural–Legal Rights. This background of the work will be explained in Chapter Three.

is rather well modeled by Article 1 of UDHR, which states, *"All human beings are born free and equal in dignity and rights."* This suggests the root element represented by "life" stands for both freedom and equal dignity and rights.

Indeed, as far as this model is concerned, the two factors of *liberty* and *equal dignity and rights* are inherently present within it. In fact, removing either of these factors will completely demolish the model.

Having said that, it is arguable that liberty is more fundamental to the model since it is more directly present within the root element of life. However, from a social perspective, liberty cannot be guaranteed, unless it is accepted that everyone has equal dignity and rights. Thus, the more nuanced view is that both *freedom* and *equal dignity and rights* are equally necessary, at least if we are to have a viable Constitutional model.

B. Building Up:
The Pursuit of Complementary Rights

The second part of the model is composed of complementary elements added to the root element. Although these elements cannot claim to improve the root element's inherent quality, they are meant to protect and increase the space available for the root element to operate in. Indeed, in protective parlance, the complementary elements can be thought of as fortifications erected around the root element.

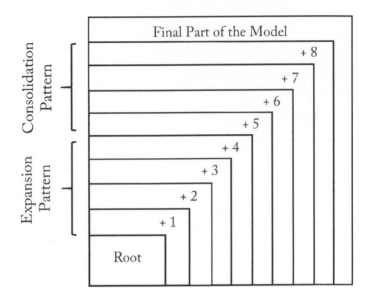

Fig-1—Structure of the Model

Figure 1 shows how the addition of each new element creates a larger set containing all earlier elements, eventually containing the whole model. The second part of the model consists of the eight elements in the middle, which can be grouped into two patterns of four elements each: the initial expansion pattern and the later consolidation pattern. The next two discussions will cover these two patterns in detail. For now, let us understand more about the complementary elements.

Each additional element is termed *complementary* because each one enables some new functionality that the earlier elements had been building toward but could not attain without the extra element being added to the mix. It is critical to note that these additional elements cannot have an adversarial relationship with any of the earlier elements. If there was such an adversarial relationship, it would imply the eventual failure of the model due to its internal contradictions.

This absence of internal contradictions is essentially the constitutional logic that is used to build this model. Obviously, this does not meet with mathematical standards, but as we shall see, it serves well enough to choose some options over others.

To bring the above logical or structural description of the model in line with the goal of individual liberty and rights, from here onward the complementary elements are termed as *Complementary Rights*, or as just *Rights* for the sake of simplicity.

However, these Rights are qualitatively different from most other human rights that are protected by documents like UDHR. Each of these Rights represents a fundamental degree of freedom, which, when taken together, gives the layout of the Constitutional structure. By contrast, the human rights paradigm of the UDHR (and other related documents) does not attempt to identify similar degrees of freedom, but rather focuses on clarifying the areas having the potential to suffer some abuse, so that those areas can be legally defended if the situation calls for it.

Initial Expansion of the Model (Initial Four Rights)

Let us now look at the initial expansion of the model, which is composed of the first four Rights (shown in Figure 1). The first Right is the negative version of the Golden Rule, which requires us to avoid harming others, and the second Right is the positive version of the Golden Rule, which requires us to help others.

These first two Rights, termed the Claim-Right and Help-Right, are reflected in the Hippocratic Oath, commonly attributed to the ancient Greek physician, Hippocrates. A portion of the oath is translated as, "*I will...benefit my patients according to my greatest ability and judgment, and*

I will do no harm or injustice to them."[4] Another segment in the same oath goes on to state, *"Into whatsoever houses I enter, I will enter to help the sick, and I will abstain from all intentional wrongdoing and harm."*

Crucially, while the first Right of avoiding harm is mandatory, the second Right of helping others is voluntary. Incidentally, the early Chinese philosopher Mencius puts the positive Golden Rule as, *"Try your best to treat others as you would wish to be treated yourself."*[5] Perhaps the spirit of the Golden Rules is also adequately conveyed by the early nineteenth century reformer William Wilberforce: *"Let everyone regulate his conduct...by the golden rule of doing to others as in similar circumstances we would have them do to us, and the path of duty will be clear."*

From a visual perspective, the first two Rights fill the spaces present in the two bottom rows of Figure 2. In particular, while the Claim-Right creates only the space on the right of the bottom row (the space on the left belongs to the root element), the Help-Right creates two new functional spaces in the row immediately above the bottom row.

---

[4] The translation is by W. H. S. Jones.

[5] In contrast to the view of Mencius, which we can use as a proxy for the voluntary Help-Right, we need to look at the Confucian view of the negative Golden Rule in a more careful manner, since its precise formulation might be disproportionally influential in the model. For the record, D. C. Lau translates the negative Golden Rule given by Confucius as, *"Do not impose on others what you yourself do not desire,"* and Raymond Dawson translates the same as, *"Do not inflict on others what you yourself would not wish done to you."*

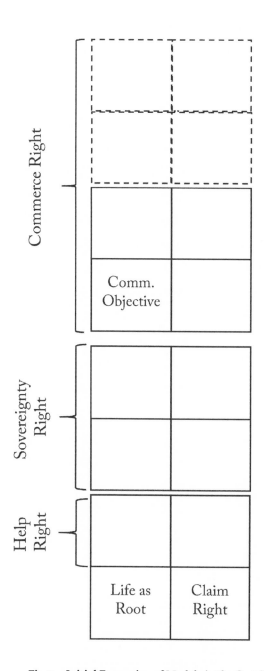

Fig-2—Initial Expansion of Model via the first four Rights

With regard to the two spaces created by the Help-Right, the left side represents the *Liberty* side of the Help, while the right side represents the *Claim* side of the same Help. The Claim present in the Help is perhaps the promise extended to the other person so that the Help can take place with more ease.

As an indirect verification of the second Right and its voluntary nature, it is possible to cite once more Article 1 of UDHR: "*All human beings are born free and equal in dignity and rights. They are endowed with reason and conscience and should act towards one another in a spirit of brotherhood.*" Note that the concepts of freedom and equal rights are invoked first and unambiguously, while brotherhood is brought up later, more as a desirable item than as a compulsory mandate.[6]

The third Right, termed the Sovereignty-Right, is indicated by the African independence leader Kwame Nkrumah: "*No people without a government of their own can expect to be treated on the same level as people of independent sovereign states. It is far better to be free to govern or misgovern yourself than to be governed by anybody else.*" As shown in Figure 2, four extra spaces are created as part of the Sovereignty-Right.[7] Obviously, this is an increase from the two spaces created by the Help-Right, and the lone space created by the Claim-Right. Clearly, the initial expansion pattern can be understood as a *doubling* of the functional spaces at each new level.

---

[6] In this regard, the position of UDHR is much better than the dictum, "Liberty, Equality, and Fraternity" since the slight collectivistic connotation of the term *fraternity* can confuse the meaning of its preceding term, *equality*. In contrast, UDHR takes care to emphasize that it is the equality of rights that is absolute.

[7] It must be mentioned here that an alternate sequencing of Rights is possible, where the Commerce-Right appears in the third spot instead of the Sovereignty-Right. This alternate sequencing of Rights will be examined in the second book of this series with the help of a quote from Martin Luther King, Jr. The second book will also quote the linguist Ferdinand de Saussure on another related point. Thus, these two people are just as important to this overall work as the people already quoted in this book.

The lower left space within the Sovereignty-Right represents the liberty of the people, in that people can come together to decide their affairs. The lower-right space represents the Claim of the people, in that people's Rights at the lower levels cannot be violated. The upper-left space represents the liberty of the people to Help people, which implies people can voluntarily join structures like the public service. The upper-right space represents the Claim present in the above Help of the people, which implies the public service structures must uphold their promise to the people.[8]

Incidentally, these four spaces created by the Sovereignty-Right correlate well with the traditional understanding of human rights, since the lower-right and upper-right spaces could be taken to represent negative rights and positive rights, respectively.

Also, the human rights' view goes further than Nkrumah does, and tries to ensure that the government will not misgovern. For instance, the preamble to the UDHR states, *"Whereas it is essential, if man is not to be compelled to have recourse, as a last resort, to rebellion against tyranny and oppression, that human rights should be protected by the rule of law."* However, just as Nkrumah warns, bad actors from outside the country could foster violence within the country in the name of human rights, while their true motive may be geopolitical. To sum up this complex situation, while *human rights* is the goal and *rule of law* is the means, *sovereignty* is the inevitable initial step on that long journey. Essentially, both Nkrumah and UDHR are correct. Nkrumah warns against foreign interference, while UDHR recognizes the people's right to demand better governance.

---

[8] Since such a promise will be valued by the people only if it is justiciable, this particular work limits it to the three parameters of cost, honesty, and quality. We shall examine these areas in detail in the following chapters.

The fourth Right is the Commerce-Right, and its bottom-up aspect is best understood from the Austrian-British economist F. A. Hayek: *"It is because every individual knows little and in particular, because we rarely know which of us knows best, that we trust the independent and competitive efforts of the many to induce the emergence of what we shall want when we see it."* If we refer to Figure 2, this bottom-up view of Commerce-Right covers only the four lower spaces present within the eight spaces created by Commerce-Right. For instance, the root's bottom-left space is now inhabited by a *commercial-objective*.

To complete our understanding of the Commerce-Right, Hayek's bottom-up perspective needs to be balanced with a top-down perspective. The need for the top-down perspective is brought out by the pioneer of political economy Adam Smith: *"People of the same trade...meet together...the conversation ends in a conspiracy against the public, or in some contrivance to raise the prices."*[9] Smith's observation, if true even to a small degree, leaves no option but to ensure that the upper half of the commercial space is kept under people's top-down control. This is necessary to avoid possible misbehaviors that could emanate from an ungoverned commercial space.

In other words, there is no independent sovereignty in the upper half of the commercial spaces. Instead, the uppermost four spaces are placed under the control of the third Sovereignty-Right. The broken lines in Figure 2 signal this key feature. As we shall see next, this control over the upper half of the commercial spaces is achieved via the remaining four Rights in the model, which form the later consolidation pattern present in the model.

---

[9] Lest this be seen as being overly harsh on the private sector, it ought to be noted that the public sector is much more inefficient than the private sector and that the demand in the public sector is usually for a rent of some kind.

Later Consolidation of the Model (Four Later Rights)

Now that we have described the first four Rights that make up the initial expansion of the model, we can investigate the later consolidation of the model that comprises the next four Rights. Since the first four Rights occupy all the functional spaces in Figure 2, we need new functional spaces to describe the remaining Rights. Figure 3 and Figure 4 are introduced here for this purpose.

The fifth Right, which is termed the Regulation-Right, can be understood from James Madison, who is generally regarded as the father of the US Constitution: *"the great difficulty lies in this: you must first enable the government to control the governed; and in the next place oblige it to control itself."* As shown in Figure 3, each space in the two outer columns, created by this Regulation-Right, is meant to regulate the functional space that lies adjacent to it.[10]

Since this is close to a doubling of the existing spaces, it may seem like the fifth Regulation-Right is continuing with the initial expansion of the model, but it would be more accurate to view it as regulating the lower-level functional spaces. In other words, rather than continuing to expand, it consolidates the functioning of the model. For instance, although the fifth Right creates two new columns on either side of the existing functional spaces, such that they mirror the existing structure of the lower-level functional spaces, it also creates four additional spaces that lie next to the newly created column on the right. Thus, the

---

[10] This is how *"enable the government to control the governed"* is realized. In this model, the *governed* are not thought of as people themselves, but rather the functional spaces that are created by the people. As an immediate consequence, the role of regulators becomes evident, which *"oblige it to control itself."* Of course, Madison probably arrived at his position by thinking about controlling people's passions and elevating their reason. In his words, *"it is reason, alone, of the public, that ought to control and regulate the government. The passions ought to be controlled and regulated by the government."*

pattern associated with the fifth Right is not the doubling observed in the first four Rights, but something else.

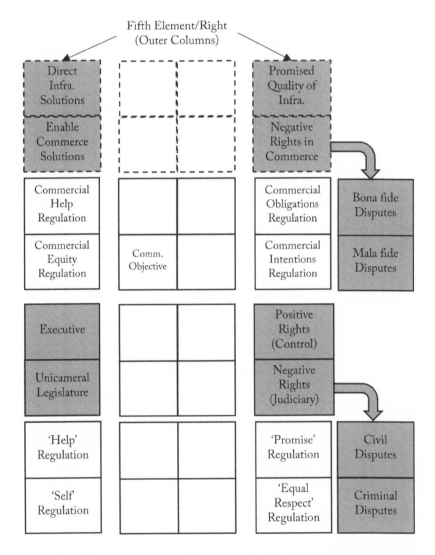

Fig-3—Regulation-Right creates the new outer columns

The unshaded spaces present in the outer columns cannot be interfered with by governments, as they are the natural regulators that evolution has placed within individuals. The four shaded spaces placed above them in the next two rows are meant to regulate the sovereign public spaces belonging to the people. These spaces are termed as *empowered-regulators*, as they are empowered for performing their regulatory function by the people.

The four lower empowered-regulators (lying next to the sovereign spaces) control their analogues in the four upper empowered-regulators, the ones with the broken boundaries. While regulators on the lower left—Legislature and Executive—are relatively free to choose their priorities, regulators on the lower right—Judiciary and Control—are meant to resolve complaints. This makes the functional spaces on the right justiciable,[11] whereas the ones on the left are not.

Since the natural regulators have no adequate structure for resolving complaints, dispute-resolution structures are created adjacent to them, which are the four spaces beyond the rightmost column of the model. At the lower levels, these spaces correspond to people's complaints in criminal and civil categories; at the higher levels, they correspond to complaints in *mala fide* and *bona fide* categories.

The difference between the two empowered-regulators on the lower right—Judiciary and Control—is crucial. While the Judiciary deals only with negative rights, the Control-function deals only with positive rights. Negative rights require *mandatory state inaction* with respect to the citizens, which leads to the description *negative rights in commerce* in the analogous position at the commerce level. Positive rights require *mandatory state*

---

[11] This *justiciable* position is used in Chapter Three to narrow down the responsibilities of the Control-function. For now, it can be noted that the role of *Ombudsman*, which is now widely accepted all over the world, clearly overlaps with the Control-function.

action in a select few areas that are identified by the citizens, which leads to the description *promised quality of infra.* in the analogous position at the commerce level.

The commonality between the Control and Judiciary functions is that they both must operate independent of the government of the day. Indeed, special provisions should definitely be made in the Constitution for ensuring that there can be no collusion between these regulators and the government.

Now that we have discussed the fifth Right, the remaining three Rights in this grouping can be examined. The commercial spaces at the fourth level have been left out of Figure 4 purely to make things easier for the reader. Including them would only have made things seem unnecessarily complicated.

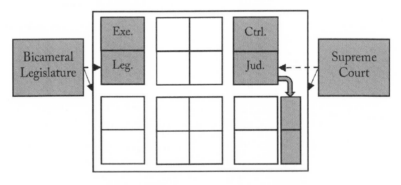

Fig-4—Later Consolidation of Model via Bicameral Legislature and Supreme Court

The sixth Right, which we call the Unification-Right, consolidates all the regulators created by the fifth Right into a Constitutional structure that works. In order to achieve this Unification, it posits two *unification-regulators*, namely the Bicameral Legislature and the Supreme Court, which can be seen on either side of Figure 4.

At the structural level, while Bicameral Legislature delegates to the regulators on the left, Supreme Court delegates to the regulators on the right. Supreme Court also has a veto over the regulators on the left, if they violate some Constitutional provisions. Regarding the arrows in Figure 4, while the normal arrows indicate the structural powers of delegation and veto enjoyed by the unification-regulators, the dashed arrows point to the fifth-level regulators—Legislature and Judiciary—which are a necessary part of their respective unification-regulators.

Having mentioned this power of delegation of the unification-regulators, it must also be noted that it is the people who delegate to the unification-regulators, and not the other way around. In particular, this means the natural regulators cannot be interfered with by the unification-regulators or any of the other regulators.

While the South American liberator Simon Bolivar's quote, "*Do not adopt the best system of government, but the one most likely to succeed,*" gives the rough position at the level of the Unification-Right, it perhaps leaves a lot of room for interpretation. Fortunately, the American jurist Wesley Hohfeld's legal analysis makes the situation at this level quite clear, by providing the logical justification for the Supreme Court's ability to veto the Legislature on Constitutional grounds. We shall briefly review Hohfeld's theory in Chapter Three.

The seventh Right, which is termed the Amendment-Right, introduces the people's ability to incorporate changes into the Constitution. While the Bicameral Legislature interprets wishes of the people at the Constitutional level, the Supreme Court ensures Constitutional changes do not have inbuilt contradictions. Since Amendments are important events, both the Bicameral Legislature and the Supreme Court may need to be bound by special procedures to give their actions more weight.

This seventh level can be understood from a noted opponent of the French Revolution, Edmund Burke, who is also generally regarded as the philosophical founder of conservatism: "*A state without the means of some change is without the means of its conservation.*" More details about the amendment capacity cannot be given here, because it reaches full maturity only in the *developmental extension* of the model. This extension of the model will be discussed shortly in this chapter.

The eighth Right, which is the Enactment-Right, enables new laws to be brought into force by the Bicameral Legislature, provided they are not in violation of the Constitutional provisions. Some flaws would be unavoidable in these new laws since it is characteristic of all human activities. However, this imperfect implementation of ideas via enactments should be thought of as a welcome situation since it justifies our ability to make corrections later. Indeed, as per Simon Bolivar, "*To do something right, it must be done twice. The first time instructs the second.*"[12]

Notably, while the Unification- and Amendment-Rights have the dual responsibility of being both conceptual and legal, the later Enactment-Right is almost entirely legal in nature. In other words, the Enactment-Right limits itself to the practical workings of the already built-up Constitutional structure and does not concern itself with any conceptual additions to the structure.

In case the reader wants a quick summary of the eight Rights, they are mentioned in Table 1,[13] along with the key characteristic that they bring to the model.

---

[12] This quote is taken from a letter Bolivar wrote to Sucre in 1823.

[13] Since the Amendment and Commerce-Right achieve full maturity only later as part of the developmental extension of the model, they are the only Rights shown in italics in Table 1.

	Table 1 Complementary Rights in the Model	
	Rights	**Remarks**
1	Claim-Right	Creates an additional functional space
2	Help-Right	Creates two new functional spaces
3	Sovereignty-Right	Creates four new functional spaces
4	*Commerce-Right*	Creates eight new functional spaces
5	Regulation-Right	Consolidates existing functional spaces by regulating them
6	Unification-Right	Consolidates existing functions by unifying them via the Constitution
7	*Amendment-Right*	Consolidates existing functions by amending the Constitution
8	Enactment-Right	Consolidates existing functions by enacting laws

While this concludes our discussion of the second part of the model, the third part of the model with its final ninth element is yet to be discussed. Let us examine this next.

C. Finishing Up:
People's Feedback as the Final Element

Since the ninth Right should be complementary to the model as a whole, it is proposed that people's feedback should be this final Right present in the model. This is because it is people's opinion about the *de facto* situation on the ground, which should cause changes in the *de jure* situation of existing laws in a nonviolent manner. Thus, the feedback element is a direct projection from the root element of life itself.

It needs to be said here that this feedback is much more than what is popularly understood as democracy. After all, people's feedback affects not just the election of representatives, but also the regulation of all four of the sovereignty spaces. Admittedly, the more visible and immediate impact is on the left side of the sovereignty spaces, especially on the representatives present in the Legislature. Obviously, it is this influence of the people over the Legislature that eventually translates into appropriate changes in the laws.

However, lest we forget, since this feedback element must be complementary to the model that has been built up so far, it must also be capable of mapping directly to the model. In order to validate this mapping capability, it is necessary to use a quote about *reform* from the chief architect of Indian Constitution, B. R. Ambedkar.

People's Feedback as Complementary to the Model

Obviously, people's feedback is to be understood as their attempt at *reform*, and according to B. R. Ambedkar, *"Reason and morality are the two most powerful weapons in the armory of a reformer. To deprive him of the use of these weapons is to disable him for action."*

Since *morality* (in this model) is represented by the two Golden Rules, it can also be understood as mapped to the first four Rights of the model. After all, the Sovereignty-Right and the Commerce-Right are extrapolated from the initial spaces created by the first two Rights. Similarly, *reason* can be understood as mapped to the later consolidation of the model, achieved by the four later Rights. After all, these later Rights deal directly with the various aspects of regulation.

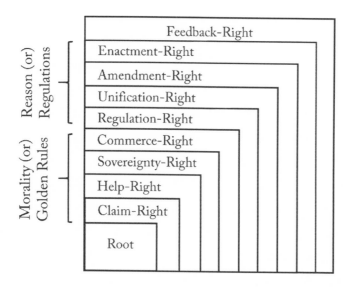

Fig-5—Mapping to Ambedkar's "Reform" (i.e., morality & reason)

This mapping of morality and reason onto the two patterns of expansion and consolidation is shown in Figure 5. Notably, Figure 5 gives a more detailed view of Figure 1, as it adds relevant descriptive information to what is essentially the same diagram.

Feedback-Right Integrated into the Model

Although it seems like Ambedkar's two reform factors can map people's feedback onto the model adequately, a more precise understanding of the mechanism by which the outermost feedback layer interacts with the inner layers is required. For instance, although the spaces belonging to the Help-Right are considered a part of *morality*, people's democratic feedback cannot be thought of as mandatorily influencing those spaces. Obviously, the spaces of the Help-Right solely depend on the individual's own voluntary choice.

To overcome shortcomings like these, the Feedback-Right needs to be understood in such a way that it integrates into the model's public spaces in a more granular manner. Incidentally, this more granular integration is also necessary to highlight the fact that the model cannot consider all democracies as legitimate expressions of its Rights-based logic; some democracies may have insufficient Constitutional safeguards built into their workings.

In order to do this, it helps that nonviolence is an implicit assumption within the model from the start. To be specific, the idea of nonviolence follows necessarily from the concept of not being adversarial to the lower order elements, for the lowermost element present in the model is the root element of life.

Although the above concept of nonviolence can be understood from the Indian independence leader and political ethicist Mahatma Gandhi— *"Nonviolence is the greatest force at the disposal of mankind. It is mightier than the mightiest weapon of destruction devised by the ingenuity of man"*[14]— this work tries to argue for a position where nonviolence is seamlessly incorporated into the Constitutional structure. In order to do that, we need to approach the concept from a different angle. Fortunately, a quote on nonviolence from Hannah Arendt, an important political theorist of the twentieth century, becomes applicable here: *"the distinction between violent and nonviolent actions is that the former is exclusively bent upon the destruction of the old, and the latter is chiefly concerned with the establishment of something new."*

Going by Arendt's quote, even the legitimate case of revoking a long-defunct law may qualify as violent. An action to abrogate a law can

---

[14] Mahatma Gandhi. "The Power of Non-violence." https://www.mkgandhi.org/nonviolence/phil2.htm (Last accessed on May 3, 2022).

be considered as nonviolent, only if a reasoned debate *"chiefly concerned with the establishment of something new"* precedes such an action. It should be noted that the criterion of *reasoned debate* suggested just above is not present in Arendt's original quote, and so it has to be treated as an additional assumption.

While this criterion of reasoned debate can be interpreted in many ways, this discussion is obviously limited to the narrow context of government and the laws enabled by it. Therefore, in the context of governance, it is proposed that the criterion of reasoned debate can be considered as met, only if the two conditions proposed by James Madison for good governments hold: *"A dependence on the people is, no doubt, the primary control on the government; but experience has taught mankind the necessity of auxiliary precautions."*[15]

While the first criterion in Madison's quote can be taken to mean that government must be run as per the wishes of the people, the second criterion implies that government must operate under a *separation of powers* doctrine. This would suggest that a democratic government with the power to revoke laws, which is certainly necessary for all governments, can be considered as a *nonviolent democracy* only if it has an effective separation of powers in its governance mechanism.

To be more specific about this situation, democratic forces might become violent if the checks and balances within it are insufficient to deliver an effective separation of powers as envisaged by the two unification-regulators present in the later consolidation of the model. Such a democracy cannot be considered as a legitimate expression of this model, for it would have a poor self-correction capacity.

---

[15] Incidentally, this remark comes in the very next sentence following the quote, which has already been included in this work for understanding the Regulation-Right. Both remarks are from *Federalist*, no. 51.

While this ends our discussion of the Constitutional model's structure, developmental extension of the model has not yet been discussed. This will be examined next.

2. DEVELOPMENTAL EXTENSION

It is necessary to discuss the developmental extension of the model because some aspects of the system gradually grow and become distinct enough to deserve a more detailed treatment. In particular, since this developmental extension is limited to the functioning of commercial organizations, it differs from the earlier model only with regard to the commercial spaces and the associated regulatory spaces.

These developmental changes are mentioned as *organizational spaces* in Figure 6 (bracket on the top left). Without those changes in the upper spaces, the diagram is merely combining the functional spaces of Figure 3 and Figure 4.

This description of developmental extension examines things from the bottom-up and top-down perspectives. It may be recalled this dual style of description was also used earlier while introducing the underlying Commerce-Right, where we used Hayek's and Smith's quotes to make two separate points.

Here, the bottom-up perspective looks at the eight lower spaces in the organizational spaces, and the top-down perspective examines the control exerted by the people over the eight upper spaces in the organizational spaces.

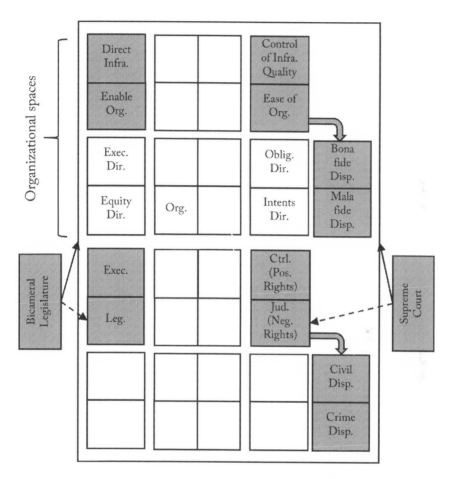

Fig-6—Developmental extension of Model via Organizational spaces
(shown by bracket on top left)

A. Bottom-Up Perspective of Organizations

Obviously, if organizations cannot arise in a country, commerce will remain at the level of direct informal interactions among its people. Once we have organizations, the major difference from the earlier model is that the so-called *commercial organization* replaces the earlier *commercial-objective*.

Further, Hayek's quote may be construed as saying that governments should avoid funding or setting up these organizations, and should instead focus on creating an enabling environment for their rise. After all, Hayek argues for trusting the *independent and competitive efforts of the many*, as opposed to the actions of a single agent.

The unshaded, regulatory spaces in the organizational spaces deal with the regulation capability that should be present within all organizations, which brings in the subject area of organizational boards. Intent and Obligations are suggested as the two major functions of Independent Directors. Just as people have their commercial complaints split into two categories, boards will also have to use the same categorization in their dispute-resolution structures. If there are complaints against an organization, it may imply the concerned board members could not satisfactorily perform their duties.

Failure at the level of the Intent Director will lead to *mala fide* disputes, which are rather serious disputes since they arise only when the organization acts in a fashion that is not in alignment with the negative Golden Rule (understood in the organizational context). In practical terms, these disputes will cover any commercial activity that could be termed as *illegal*. After all, if something cannot be termed as illegal, it will be rather hard to raise that matter in a court of law.[16] In theoretical terms, Golden Rules in the commercial context may be viewed as primarily aimed at helping customers, provided the laws of the state and the rights of citizens are not violated.

---

[16] It is up to the people and their representatives to ensure that the law sufficiently covers all the possible organizational chicaneries that might be attempted. If this seems rather difficult to achieve in practice, proportionally great care will have to be given to the role played by Intent Directors.

In contrast to *mala fide* disputes, *bona fide* disputes arise because of failures at the level of the Obligations Director. These disputes are less serious in nature, as they deal only with disagreements over voluntary interactions. Basically, this category mostly boils down to disputes the organization may have with its customers, partners, and employees. The focus in this category of disputes should be on processes that allow for quick resolutions outside the courtroom; otherwise, the courts could get clogged.

In addition, we can use quotes from Eleanor Roosevelt and Ayn Rand to further characterize the bottom-up approach within the organizational spaces. Eleanor Roosevelt was the chair of the committee that drafted the UDHR, and Ayn Rand was a Russian-American writer and philosopher. According to Eleanor Roosevelt, *"Happiness is not a goal, it is a by-product. Paradoxically, the one sure way not to be happy is deliberately to map out a way of life in which one would please oneself completely and exclusively."* This position is seemingly bluntly contradicted by Ayn Rand in her fictional work *The Fountainhead*, when her main character says, *"But I don't think of you."* However, the two perspectives are complementary from the vantage point of the entrepreneur.

The two perspectives can be mapped onto the lower spaces within the organizational spaces of Figure 6, with Rand's quote on the lower row and Roosevelt's on the upper row. While Rand's quote may refer to the need to be free of unnecessary regulations and having the freedom to ignore those market segments that cannot be the focus of the commercial organization, Roosevelt's quote may refer to the need to please customers who are the focus of the commercial organization.

Although it is probably only Rand who had entrepreneurs on her mind while producing her works, it is likely that most successful entrepreneurs will agree with the positions espoused by both of them. If entrepreneurs don't incorporate both views, namely that of ignoring unviable market segments and working hard to please their target customers, it is difficult to see them becoming successful in their endeavors.

However, when the commercial activities of organizations gradually grow, it is necessary to add the perspective of others in society through the introduction of Independent Directors. Without the restraint brought in by these Directors, larger organizations could easily cause unintentional harm to the people through their large-scale activities in the environment.

Finally, some organizations may also take part in the uppermost row of Figure 6, if they decide to take part in the country's infrastructural activities. Obviously, only the board can decide whether an organization will take part in the country's infrastructural areas. If a commercial organization takes part in these top-down infrastructural initiatives, it may be termed as an *infra-organization*. These infra-organizations can be understood as playing a role similar to that of public servants at the sovereignty level.

B. Top-Down Perspective of People

It may be recalled that the need for people controlling the upper commercial spaces was justified by using a quote from Adam Smith. Obviously, that concern of Smith would also call for keeping the upper organizational spaces under the control of the people. This can only be achieved if organizations are prevented from exercising undue influence on the government.

This need to ensure that the governance space belongs solely to the people can also be gleaned from the well-known address given by

Abraham Lincoln, the American President who led his country during the American Civil War: *"that government of the people, by the people, for the people shall not perish from the earth."* Consequently, the emphasis must be on regulation of organizations, by the people and for the people (not regulation by and for organizations).[17]

In connection with this, although Figure 3 requires that negative rights must exist in the space of an individual's commerce, Figure 6 does not necessarily require that organizational rights exist in a similarly strict manner. Notably, Figure 6 only allows for *ease of organizational solutions* in the space of negative rights. This is mostly because organizational spaces arise only as a developmental extension from the individual spaces. Therefore, organizational spaces cannot be treated at par with the human spaces.

Also, the Amendment-Right is thought to mature to its full capacity only as part of the developmental extension. This mature understanding of the Amendment-Right is given by the noted Indian Supreme Court Justice H. R. Khanna: *"Although it is permissible under the power of amendment to effect changes...and to adapt the system to the requirement of changing conditions, it is not permissible...to alter the basic institutional pattern."*[18] This basically means that the Judiciary must not be complicit in the Constitution's destruction.

---

[17] This calls for the US Supreme Court decision in *Citizens United* to be revisited, since it allows for entities other than individuals to fund election campaigns and, thus, influence public policy in a disproportional manner. Since organizations are artificial constructs created as per the wishes of the people, people should regulate them (not the other way around).

[18] Although Justice Khanna is speaking of the case *Kesavananda Bharati* here, this model cannot support that verdict. A model cannot take a firm position on any specific Constitution, as it is limited to a more constrained general interpretation based on conceptual reasoning.

If an amendment wants to remove indispensable norms like democracy or rule of law, it is the duty of the Judiciary to disavow the move, even if the immediate practical result might be their impeachment. Notably, Justice Khanna's *basic institutional pattern* can be understood as an advanced take on Wesley Hohfeld's immunity right, such that immunity refers to a scholarly understanding of the minimum Constitutional position.

It is probably necessary to give the gist of Hohfeld's theory here, so the reader can understand the concept of *immunity*. To put it briefly, while people are *liable* to the *power* of the Legislature, they also have *immunity* from that *power* because of the Constitution. If the regulators on the left side of the model are power-regulators, and those on the right are immunity-regulators, the Supreme Court would be an immunity-regulator. It would be charged with defending the people's immunity, especially with regard to a minimum Constitutional structure.

A rudimentary attempt toward understanding such a minimum Constitutional structure is presented in this work. Obviously, it needs to be reviewed by legal and Constitutional experts, so that the mistakes that are sure to be present in it can be removed.

3. DOMINANCE OF BOTTOM-UP FORCES

Having discussed theoretical aspects about human rights and the Constitutional structure, it is probably necessary to add a cautionary practical note regarding the modern-world economy. The world desperately needs to achieve major breakthroughs in sustainable energy if it is to handle the coming environmental challenges. Without enabling developments in the energy sector, it is likely that this model, and others like it, will be of little consequence with regard to the future developments in the area of human rights.

On a more academic note, this model is premised on a framework that clearly places bottom-up forces in the dominant role. In fact, the bottom-up forces are seen as giving rise to some subsidiary forces, which might be described as top-down by some observers, but which are still under the indirect control of complex bottom-up mechanisms. So, it would not be incorrect to say that bottom-up forces are running every aspect of the model. Actually, their influence is being greatly understated when they are described as just *dominant* over top-down forces.

Thus, although the aim of this work is to model the Constitutional structure, it seems as though that will be possible only if the real, underlying aim is to protect and increase people's liberty space, as that is what allows us to tap into their bottom-up forces.[19]

---

[19] This is the reason why Nelson Mandela's quote about freedom is placed right at the start. Among the quotes shared in this work, Mandela's comes closest to capturing the spirit of the bottom-up forces. The overall model follows more or less in a straight-forward manner from that thinking.

2

Separation of Powers
and Rule of Law

Since the structure of the Constitutional model has been discussed, we can examine two of its important features. First, the model's structure seems to capture a four-step evolutionary progress within societies. This will lead us to an understanding of the separation of powers doctrine. Second, the model's structure shows a very strong privacy protection regime within it. This will lead us to an understanding concerning the rule of law. These two areas are addressed respectively in the two sections of this chapter.

1. EVOLUTIONARY STAGES TO SEPARATION OF POWERS

This first section on separation of powers has three main parts. We start by looking at the four evolutionary stages associated with the model. Next, we look at the bottlenecks (i.e., evolutionary culs-de-sac) that have to be overcome for achieving stability at each evolutionary stage. Thereafter, we inspect the regulatory mechanisms (i.e., separation of powers) that seem necessary if we are to achieve an adequate amount of stability at each evolutionary stage.

A. Evolutionary Stages

When it comes to the evolutionary stages, we can lay out the four stages sequentially and connect each of the stages to the regulatory mechanisms. This would essentially create Figure 7a, with two rows and four boxes in each row.

As mentioned in the boxes present in the upper row, Stage-I deals with the *natural* space of people, where governments cannot enter.[20] This space is modeled by the root element of life, Claim-Right, Help-Right, and natural regulation capacity present in these functional areas. Stage-II deals with the *feudal* dynamics typically seen in history. It covers Sovereignty-Right, Commerce-Right, and a poorly developed regulation capacity of those areas.

Stage-III deals with the *democratic* dynamics of modern Constitutional democracies. It covers all the later Rights in the model, especially the Feedback-Right of the people. However, the commercial organization space is still poorly developed at the third stage. Stage-IV deals with the *developmental* dynamics of economics. This last stage, which is basically the developmental extension described in the previous chapter, gradually

---

[20] If a government enters this space, it would be like violating the dictum used in the medical area, where the mandate is to "*First, do no harm.*" In the words of Florence Nightingale, "*It may seem a strange principle to enunciate as the very first requirement in a hospital that it should do the sick no harm.*"

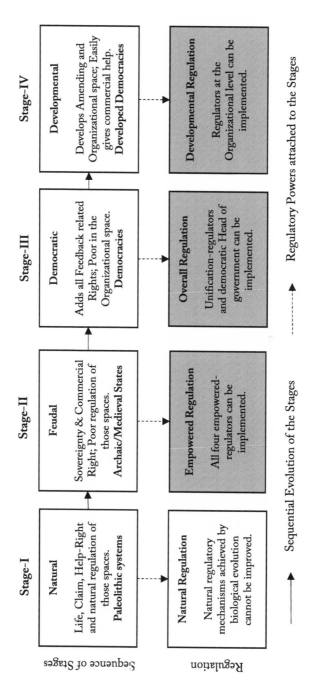

Fig-7a—Evolution of Social Systems across the Four Stages

achieves a developed economy, mostly via a mature approach to commercial organizations.

The upper row gives the details of the sequential evolutionary stages, and the lower row gives the details of the regulation present at each level.

In other words, Stage-I deals with people's private matters, like personal and religious values; Stage-II deals with people's sovereignty but with an unfortunate bias for authoritarian and top-down forces; Stage-III deals with the balancing bottom-up feedback coming from the people; and Stage-IV deals with the achievement of sustainable economic prosperity.

Although each stage is associated with specific regulatory mechanisms, achieving full maturity in any given stage is not mandatory for the system to progress to the next stage. Achieving maturity in the regulation of each stage becomes essential only later, when there is an urgent need to sustain all the sophisticated advances achieved by society as part of Stage-IV.

This is partly why the Amendment space can reach its full development only in the final stage. Had it fully developed at an earlier stage, there would have been no need for any later stage, as all the necessary information would have become available for the system. Therefore, although both commerce and amendment areas are present early on in the model, they become fully developed only as part of the developmental extension.

Most importantly, while the regulations of Stage-II, III, and IV can be improved *post facto*, the natural regulation connected with Stage-I cannot be improved. Obviously, if there are flaws inherent in humanity, they cannot be removed without being in fundamental violation of human rights. By contrast, achieving an effective democracy definitely requires the regulation of Stage-III to be adequately improved.

This is why the introductory remarks in Chapter One emphasized that the model is only for improving the public space of the people. Private spaces cannot be improved by this model. Instead, society depends on the pro-social and cooperative behavior encouraged by religious and other family traditions, so that the spaces present as part of Stage-I are adequately supportive of democratic and economic activities. The basic argument that can be put forward is about a synergistic relationship between the private and public spaces, which can increase people's liberty.

Perhaps the first three stages have largely been anticipated by the political economists Daron Acemoglu and James Robinson in their book, *Why Nations Fail*. In that work, they characterize countries as progressing through three distinct levels. The lack of political centralization characterizes the first level. However, once political centralization is achieved, the next level is controlled by the presence of *extractive institutions*, which tend to benefit the elite of the society. Finally, in some fortunate circumstances that depend on various historical contingencies, societies could go on to develop broad-based *inclusive institutions*, which imply a relative absence of *extractive institutions* present earlier. Clearly, these three levels described by Acemoglu and Robinson correspond closely with the first three stages of our model.

Arguably, even the final, fourth stage of our model can come under the sweeping rubric of *inclusive institutions*, but this specific point may not be implied in the thesis of the authors. The point being made here is that the hypothesis of four evolutionary stages, which is strongly supported by the structural features of the model, has at least some empirical evidence in its favor, due to completely independent research based on well-known historical records.

B. Evolutionary Culs-de-sac

While it is possible that systems could progress from the initial stages to the later stages rather quickly, such a trouble-free progress seems unlikely based on history. It appears far more probable that the systems will get stuck at some point in the overall evolutionary arc. These bottleneck situations are termed as *evolutionary culs-de-sac*, as it could become difficult to progress to the later evolutionary stages once entrenchment sets in.

Since improving the experience at the level of Stage-I is clearly outside the scope of this model, it is only possible to examine these cul-de-sac situations in relation to the later stages. To start with, Stage-II is termed *feudal* and not *tyrannical*, as the latter quality is not necessarily implied. After all, *tyrannical-rule* would be a devolution from the level of the feudal system, and therefore, it should perhaps be identified as the evolutionary cul-de-sac at the Stage-II level.

To be more specific about its character, not only does it have the extractive quality of the feudal system, but it is also far more coercive in its approach. Incidentally, tyrannical systems need not always be a single-person rule; it could also be controlled by a small, elite group at the top. In contrast to the tyrannical system, the possibility for a relatively benevolent feudal system cannot be completely discounted. An example of such a benevolent system would be the British system after the Glorious Revolution of 1688.

Just as Stage-II may not develop fully due to the presence of *tyrannical-rule*, Stage-III may also not develop fully due to the presence of *majoritarian-rule*. This latter situation is assumed to occur when the leading political faction consistently gets majoritarian vote share (i.e., greater than 50 percent) in elections. Fortunately, some protection against this situation can be achieved through the second house of Legislature.

Indeed, one of the biggest bonuses in the *federal* system is that its second house, which tends to be controlled by the constituent states, can considerably reduce the risk of majoritarian-rule at the federal center. Therefore, despite the fact that federal systems have features that lie outside this model, when federations are implemented properly, they are capable of performing at the democratic Stage-III level. The challenge for the nonfederal democratic systems is to institute some structural failsafe, such that they become at least as reliable as the federal system in their capacity to avoid the majoritarian cul-de-sac.

Just as there are problems on the road to Stage-II and Stage-III, there are problems as we move to Stage-IV as well. In particular, when a system nears the Stage-IV status, it faces a situation where power is increasingly wielded by corporates and their lobbies. Indeed, the representatives of the people begin to represent the interests of the corporates over that of the people. We may refer to this cul-de-sac as *corporate-rule*.

Basically, each cul-de-sac may be thought of as a pathological variation of the evolutionary stage. Although the culs-de-sac may seem difficult to overcome, occasional changes in the surrounding environment may sometimes give the opportunity for serious reform. On the other hand, even after successfully implementing the regulatory apparatus of a stage, there is the danger of devolving back to the cul-de-sac, especially if adequate care is not taken to maintain the regulatory apparatus.

Notably, the regulatory apparatus associated with each evolutionary stage can be understood in terms of the Constitutional separation of powers. To distinguish the structures proposed in this work from the popularly understood paradigm of separation of powers, we shall refer to it with hyphens, as *separation-of-powers*. This topic is addressed next.

C. Constitutional Separation-of-Powers

The Constitutional separation-of-powers deals only with regulating the three, latter stages. The concerned regulators at Stage-II, Stage-III, and Stage-IV are termed empowered-regulators, overall-regulators, and developmental-regulators.

If the first decent implementation of the empowered-regulators was done by the British,[21] the first relatively complete implementation of the overall-regulators was done by the US.[22] In comparison, the developmental-regulators may not have been achieved adequately anywhere. However, the scope for more clarity exists across all three of the regulators. The hope is that a variety of attempts to correct or improve this kind of structural analysis will eventually yield some useful results.

Empowered-Regulation at Stage-II

As seen in Figure 3, there are two distinct sets of empowered-regulators, with the first set adjacent to the sovereignty spaces, and the second adjacent to the public commercial spaces.[23] These regulatory spaces are highlighted via the shaded boxes for their easy identification. A notable contrast within the empowered-regulators is that, while

---

[21] It is to be noted that apart from correctly underscoring the Parliament's supremacy, British system also evolved the common law tradition, wherein the past legal positions adopted by the Judiciary are just as important as the letter of law itself. This differs from the Continental civil law tradition, where only the statutory law is important. It can be argued that many positions adopted by the model are more in line with the common law tradition.

[22] The US achievement is diluted by the compromised initiation of the US Constitution since voting was withheld from women and slaves, and bizarrely, slaves were counted as fractions of individuals.

[23] Incidentally, Chinese statesman Sun Yat-sen proposed Control Yuan and Examination Yuan, which have been rolled into the Control-function in this model.

regulators on the left can freely interpret the wishes of the people, regulators on the right can only interpret the law, such that there are no contradictions.

Empowered-regulation is the most that can be achieved when the system is essentially feudal in character, which implies the feedback of democracy is absent in the system. However, since this model proposes no way to implement the four empowered-regulators without resorting to the democracy of Stage-III, there is at present no safe way to implement or improve the Stage-II regulators by mechanisms of that level itself.

Admittedly, the gradual evolution of the British system of governance over several centuries, with its emphasis on Parliamentary supremacy, does show that it can be done, but obviously, that achievement is not easily replicable elsewhere.[24]

Overall-Regulation at Stage-III

To start with, overall-regulation can be understood in terms of the dual control exerted by the unification-regulators (Bicameral Legislature and the Supreme Court) over the empowered-regulators. This is shown in Figure 4. Although Unification-Right creates the unification-regulators at the sixth level, they do their work across all four levels that form the later consolidation of the model, which enables the self-correction in democracies at Stage-III.

---

[24] To be clear, since the feedback of democracy is present in the current British system, it should be thought of as being at least at the Stage-III level. Indeed, due to its developed economy, it might even be considered a Stage-IV system, albeit an unstable one, like all the other developed countries.

In order to move from the two unification-regulators to an understanding of the overall-regulators, we need only look at the French judge
and political philosopher Montesquieu's thesis on the three arms of
the government—Executive, Legislative, and Judiciary. While the two
unification-regulators clearly play the Legislative and Judiciary roles, the
Executive role is played by the head of government (especially in foreign
affairs). Thus, the overall-regulators are composed of three institutions
—the two unification-regulators and the head of government.

Admittedly, although Montesquieu identifies the role played by the
Bicameral Legislature, his work may not have identified the full structure
of the Supreme Court. But that criticism of incomplete scholarship can
be leveled at this model as well.[25] Having said that, this model does provide some additional information about overall-regulators. For instance,
it suggests that the two unification-regulators are senior to the head of
government, roughly in the same manner that people are senior to the
unification-regulators. After all, the causal control in the model emerges
from the bottom up.

Developmental-Regulation at Stage-IV

Developmental-regulation refers to the regulators in the organizational space. They are shown in Figure 6. Although the developmental-
regulators that parallel natural regulators cannot be interfered with by the
government, empowered-regulators at the developmental level have no
such luxury. They are controlled by the analogous empowered-regulators
present adjacent to the people's sovereignty spaces.

---

[25] This model does not give sufficient details regarding the two specializations present within the
Supreme Court. By contrast, the model is clearer on the two legislative houses within the Bicameral Legislature (discussed in later chapters).

This regulation is still rather poorly understood, as there are hardly any extant examples that can be safely emulated. Even the most developed nations have serious deficiencies in this area. For instance, the US system allows money power of commercial organizations to interfere in the functioning of government, whereas this model is quite clear that only the people should have control over government. The US system is also weak in infrastructure and white-collar crime, especially the *mala fide* issues arising at the corporate level.

However, it needs to be noted here that privately run enterprises and free-market forces are indeed the most important positions for an economy to take up and hold on to, as far as enabling prosperity for the people is concerned.

2. RULE OF LAW

Now that we have explained the model's position on the separation of powers, we can look at the rule of law. First, we describe the role of Judiciary and the nature of disputes. Second, rule-of-law present in the model (hyphenated to distinguish it from the traditional *rule of law*) is examined as part of the four empowered-regulators. Third, we contrast the need for protecting the private space against the need for public space regulators. Finally, we look at the implications from the above discussions on Stage-IV organizational privacy.

A. Judiciary and the Nature of Disputes

Judiciary exists to ensure that the negative rights of citizens are protected from abuse by the government. To start with, this certainly implies that public servants cannot interfere in the private space of the citizens.[26]

However, this is an insufficient understanding of the full breadth of negative rights. When called upon by the people, Judiciary must also protect the private space of citizens from the selfish encroachments sought by other citizens. Indeed, it is this additional duty that leads to the spaces meant for the resolution of criminal and civil disputes.[27]

Since the Claim-Right is considered mandatory, prosecution is done by the government. On the other hand, civil disputes must necessarily be escalated to the judicial system by an aggrieved party. In other words, the judicial system cannot interfere in civil disputes without the consent of at least one of the affected parties. The nature of criminal and civil disputes can also be understood from the details of Figure 8a.

Figure 8a is essentially the same as Figure 4, except that the two unification-regulators have been dropped. Notably, three of the four private spaces have been given abbreviations: NG, PG, and NP. These convey the nature of the Golden Rules that are active in those spaces. NG represents the negative version of the Golden Rule, PG represents the positive version of the Golden Rule, and NP represents a combination of

---

[26] Caution is called for while interpreting what *interference* amounts to since only the ability to influence is being thought of. For instance, mere storage of information for a limited amount of time may not amount to interference. However, the norms around the storage must be such that the data is not amenable to misuse. For instance, if there is any nonautomated attempt to access data that belongs in the private domain, the details around that attempt (like the public official involved) can be logged into a permanent record. The existence of such a record would mean that if there is any attempt to access private information without the Judiciary's consent, the concerned official could be automatically terminated by the authorities. Of course, many additional safeguards must also be built into the system, but those details cannot be suggested here, as this work is focused only on the Constitutional model.

[27] Of course, several scholars have mentioned the fact that ensuring some negative rights, like dispute resolution, will require state action from the government via institutions like the police force.

the two positions. While criminal disputes arise only at the NG level, civil disputes arise only at the NP level.

B. Rule-of-Law as Part of the Empowered-Regulators

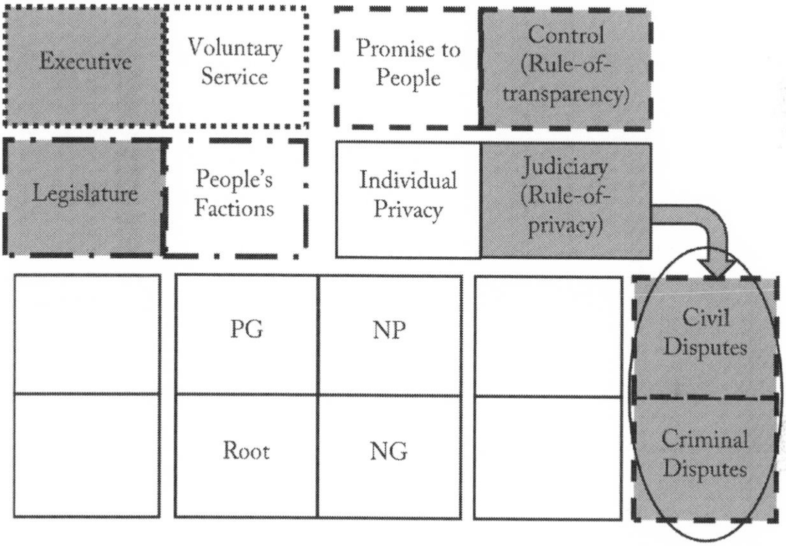

Fig-8a—Dispute Judiciary (within oval) protects privacy

When it comes to the regulatory functions responsible for the management of the four sovereign spaces, it cannot be the case that they are not connected to the concerned sovereignty spaces. This connection between the regulatory space and the associated sovereign space is shown in Figure 8a through the use of four, distinct-line styles. Basically, the Executive (dotted lines) is tied to the top-left space of *voluntary service*; Legislature (dotted and dashed lines) is tied to the bottom-left space of *people's factions*; Control (dashed lines) is tied to the top-right space of *promise to people*; and Judiciary (solid lines) is tied to the bottom-right space of *individual privacy*.

Therefore, while the bottom-right space represents the rule-of-privacy, the top-right space might represent a rule-of-transparency. While this might be an interesting way to think of the two main components present within rule-of-law, the latter concept of rule-of-transparency is more tentative than rule-of-privacy—and will be expanded upon in the next chapter.

In Figure 8a, it is notable that both the private spaces of individuals and the higher Judiciary represent the bottom-right space of individual privacy. However, the spaces for criminal or civil dispute resolution, present on the bottom right of the diagram, are thought to represent the top-right space of the Control-function. This is because, at the lower level of Judiciary, the functionaries are only concerned with proper implementation of the norms that have already been put in place, either by the higher Judiciary or the Legislature. It is perhaps only at the highest level of Judiciary that functionaries can reason whether the legislated laws violate basic principles.

C. Private Space Protection Is
More Important than the Constitution

Legislature is a more powerful regulator than the Judiciary because it decides the specifics of all the laws implemented by the Judiciary. But Legislature does not have the power (as per the model) to take away the core responsibility of the Judiciary, which is to ensure the *fundamental protection of private spaces*.

This implies that the need to protect private spaces is more important to the model than even the doctrine of Constitutional separation-of-powers. Or alternatively, the human rights paradigm represented by a UDHR-like approach is more important than the model's capacity to improve the public spaces of people.

For instance, human conscience or free will is at the heart of natural regulation present in the private space. A failure to protect this private space, from the government or organizations, will equate to a destabilization of the bottom-up stability of the social system. By contrast, failure to implement an effective separation-of-powers doctrine only implies that the system is stuck at the Stage-II level. It does not by itself threaten to make the people's private lives unstable.

D. Implication of Privacy for Stage-IV Organizations

Just as the government is not allowed to interfere in the private space of individuals, commercial organizations also cannot be allowed to interfere in that space. After all, organizations have been enabled by governments to serve the citizens better in the economic domain, not to destroy the boundaries that ought to exist around the people's private spaces. For instance, this has relevance to organizations operating in the internet area.[28]

Moreover, governments cannot be allowed to interfere in the boards of organizations, for those organizations represent the closest possible modeling of the human commercial space (while ensuring beneficial outcomes to the people). If such interference is allowed, it might create a precedent that governments could point to for interfering in the people's conscience spaces as well.

---

[28] For instance, people's private data should not leave their home jurisdictions (provided the home country is at the Stage-III level) and should not be shared with third parties. Besides, public servants (and even government agencies) should not get access to such data without a due process approval from an independent Judiciary.

For instance, the fact that the organizational space is an artificial construct may be used as a justification by governments for interfering in the organizational space. While that argument points to a legitimate distinction between the organizational and the individual spaces, it should also remind us that human, private-space activity is natural, which makes it rather distinct from the organizational space.

Further, if a government does not intend to interfere in organizations, which certainly seems to be a Stage-IV prerequisite according to the model, it should avoid owning equity in organizations, for equity ownership implies that the government can interfere in organizational boards through its nominees to the board.

A slightly separate reasoning for avoiding government ownership of equity comes from Hayek's quote, when it is understood in the organizational context. As can be recalled, the quote—*"we trust the independent and competitive efforts of the many to induce the emergence of what we shall want"*—requires that organizations be independent and competitive. However, such a condition cannot possibly exist if some faraway government is running the organization, even if only at the board level.

3. A QUICK SUMMARY

A summary of the discussions on separation-of-powers is shown in Table 2. The three rows of the table exhibit the details associated with the three evolutionary stages of Stage-II, Stage-III, and Stage-IV. In particular, each row mentions the evolutionary cul-de-sac that has to be overcome to achieve the evolutionary stage, and the separation-of-powers doctrine that is necessary for overcoming the cul-de-sac.

Table 2 Evolutionary Position of the Model		
Evolutionary Stages	Evolutionary Culs-De-Sac	Const. Separation-of-Powers
Stage-II	Tyrannical-rule	Empowered-regulation
Stage-III	Majoritarian-rule	Overall-regulation
Stage-IV	Corporate-rule	Developmental-regulation

Regarding the discussions on rule-of-law, we emphasized it implies rule-of-privacy, both at the individual and at the organizational level. While the former is sacrosanct, the latter is an artificial construct. Notably, apart from rule-of-privacy, rule-of-law also implies a need for rule-of-transparency, mostly to ensure that the sovereignty promise given to the people is not broken. Although rule-of-transparency could not be discussed at any depth in this chapter, it is among the areas discussed in the next chapter.

3

Background Theoretical Considerations

This chapter deals with the prominent theoretical considerations that were present in the background while the model was being worked on. The first section lays out the primary inspiration behind this work, namely the four theoretical distinctions present in Rights theory. The second section attempts to develop a reconciliation between this Rights-based model and the existing practice of human rights.

1. INSPIRATION FOR THE MODEL: RIGHTS DISTINCTIONS

Although the diagrammatic approach to the model was anticipated by the Stanford Encyclopedia of Philosophy's entry on the topic of Rights,[29]

---

[29] Stanford Encyclopedia of Philosophy Archive. (2005;2020). "Rights." https://plato.stanford.edu/archives/spr2021/entries/rights/ (Last accessed on May 3, 2022).

the inspiration for the model came from the four theoretical distinctions present in Rights theory.[30] The four distinctions are given below.

1. Claim–Liberty Rights
2. Negative–Positive Rights
3. Individual–Group Rights
4. Natural–Legal Rights

We shall explain each of these distinctions here.

There will also be a deep dive into four specific areas closely associated with the above distinctions. The four areas are the following: Hohfeld's theory (within Claim–Liberty Rights), Control-function (within Negative–Positive Rights), factions (within Individual–Group Rights), and medical rights (within Natural–Legal Rights). These additional discussions—especially the Control-function—are unavoidable for understanding the material presented in the following chapters.

On the whole, the expectation is that all these explanations will make clear how the four Rights distinctions influenced the framing of the model.

A. Claim–Liberty Rights

Let us start with the Claim–Liberty Rights distinction, since it is the most fundamental. It prioritizes Claim-Right first and Liberty-Right second. This is because the distinction assumes that all legal restrictions (i.e., laws) already exist and are subsumed under the rubric of *Claim*. The liberty

---

[30] Wikipedia. "Human rights." https://en.wikipedia.org/wiki/Human-rights (Last accessed on May 3, 2022).

space that is still left vacant after accounting for these existing claims is available for people to enjoy as their liberty right.

This distinction says nothing about whether the laws are ethically valid or not. It merely assumes that because the laws exist, they must not be violated. If the space of all such laws, whether currently enacted or not, is also included within the ambit of claim space, that larger space is indicated by the totality of space within Figure 9.

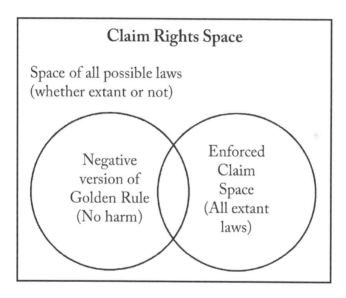

Fig-9—Claim Right Space

However, this particular model is built up by using the negative version of the Golden Rule, which is represented by the left circle in the diagram. That Golden Rule space will surely have some overlap with the existing laws represented by the right circle, but there may also be some other spaces within the existing laws that do not directly satisfy the ethical criterion of the Golden Rule.

This does not mean that the concerned laws are unethical; it may merely mean the connection is so indirect, it might as well be in another domain. Indeed, although the model starts out with the Golden Rule, it accepts the space of enacted laws as well, since that possibility has been acknowledged via the eighth Enactment-Right in the model.

Instead of looking solely at a complicated legal code to understand what can be done legally, which is the current situation, the proposed model suggests that, since the *no harm* principle is a foundation of ethics, it might serve as a foundation for law as well, at least for resolving criminal disputes.

This is in tune with the fact that the evolution of human nature preceded the arrival of codified laws of nation states. Basically, the root element of life naturally exists first, but if there is to be a peaceful coexistence with other individuals in society, each individual must take care to adhere to the society's claim space, which is a set of artificial norms created by the society.

Hohfeld's Analysis

As can be recalled, Hohfeld's analysis is referred to in the model's build-up in order to support the veto power of the Supreme Court. Since Hohfeld's analysis is inextricably tied up with Claim–Liberty Rights distinction, this is a good place to review his contribution to legal theory.

Wesley Hohfeld identified what he called *"the lowest common denominators of the law."* These are basically eight concepts, namely these: Right, Duty, No-Right, Privilege, Power, Liability, Disability, and Immunity.

Table 3 Hohfeld's Analysis of Legal Concepts				
Hohfeldian Incidents	Privilege	Right	Power	Immunity
Other Party Position	No-Right	Duty	Liability	Disability

Of these, the *Right* and *Privilege* concepts correspond respectively to the Claim-Right and Liberty-Right (i.e., space occupied by the root) of the model. *Duty* and *No-Right* can be thought of as the logical devices necessary to pin down the use of these concepts.

Basically, having a *Right* implies the other party has a *Duty* toward you. Similarly, having a *Privilege* implies the other party has a *No-Right* toward you. This relationship is said to be *jural correlatives* of each other, as the existence of one relation automatically implies the other relation for the other party. On the other hand, the relationships of *Right* vs. *No-Right* and *Duty* vs. *Privilege* are said to be *jural opposites* of each other, as they cannot both exist at the same time. Existence of one legal relation would imply the absence of the other legal relation.

The remaining four concepts, as shown in Table 3, share exactly the same relationship among themselves as the first four concepts. While Power-Liability and Immunity-Disability are jural correlatives, Power-Disability and Immunity-Liability are jural opposites. Since the relevant relationships have already been detailed in the above paragraph, it is only necessary to define the legal position of *Power* and *Immunity* to appreciate the whole framework. *Power* is the ability to alter legal relations, and *Immunity* is the freedom from the *Power* of another party.

Incidentally, the four concepts in the upper row of Table 3, namely Privilege, Right, Power, and Immunity, are known as *Hohfeldian incidents*, since these are usually the legal relations that get scrutinized. The other four concepts are more like the supporting structure built to define the Hohfeldian incidents in an appropriately clear manner. The four Hohfeldian incidents can be mapped to the model's four columns, as shown in Figure 10.[31]

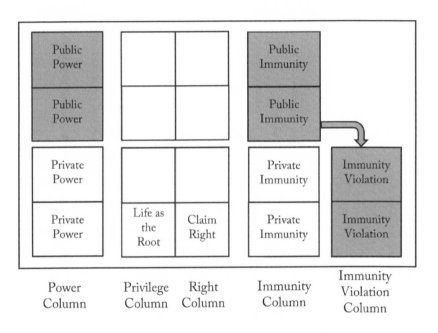

Fig-10—*Mapping the Four Hohfeldian Incidents*
onto the Model's Columns

---

[31] Incidentally, since the four Hohfeldian incidents have been mapped to the columns of the model in Figure 10, it is worth noting that the difference between Privilege-Power and Claim-Immunity might also be characterized as the difference between Active and Passive Rights, respectively. This is based on the work done by David Lyons. Active Right, which correlates with Privilege and Power, would be about "Party A has a right to do X." Passive Right, which correlates with Claim and Immunity, would be about "Party A has a right that Party B do X." In contrast to the mapping of Active and Passive Rights onto the model, the Will and Interest theories of rights (covered in Chapter Twelve) perhaps cannot be mapped onto the model, as they each claim to represent all of the rights territory by themselves.

Perhaps the legal positions associated with the simple case of using one's computer will make these legal relations more understandable to the reader. *Privilege*, which is the Liberty-Right of the model, is the right to use one's computer (or read one's book). *Right*, which is the Claim-Right of the model, would be the ability to prevent others from having the *Privilege* right over that computer. *Power* would be the right to modify the Claim-Right in some manner. *Immunity* would be the freedom from others having the *Power* right over one's computer.

Thus, the Supreme Court exists to provide citizens the *Immunity* from any unconstitutional changes to law. Even though the Legislature has the *Power* to make law, it has to respect the *Immunity* of the citizens in those areas where they have Constitutional protection.

Hohfeld's analysis is now slightly over a century old and has been extensively reviewed in legal circles.[32] Therefore, support from Hohfeld's analysis makes the later consolidation part of the model more reliable than anticipated earlier. This is because each degree of freedom in the later part (Regulate, Unify, Amend, and Enact) requires the presence of both power- and immunity-regulators.

B. Negative–Positive Rights

For understanding the scope of Negative–Positive Rights within the model, we start by looking at Figure 11, which shows the Venn diagram of the two Golden Rules. After all, it is the projection of the Golden Rules onto the sovereignty space that creates the spaces of negative and positive rights within the model.

---

[32] Also, since Hohfeld's theory is meant for the legal domain, it probably cannot be invoked prior to reaching the level of Regulation- and Unification-Rights.

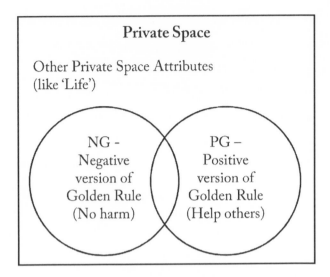

Fig-11—Private Space

The negative rights' space is projected purely from the negative Golden Rule (left circle without the intersection space). By contrast, the positive rights' space is projected from the intersection space of the two Golden Rules (and not from the right circle alone).[33] As a consequence of these structural constraints, the model can only access negative and positive rights *indirectly* as subsets within the Sovereignty-Right, rather than directly, as something that is to be done or not done by the government.

Moreover, the two interacting parties at the level of sovereignty are rather different from the Golden Rules. In the Golden Rules, it is two people who act on each other. But at the level of sovereignty, while one party can be thought of as the people, the other party is composed of voluntary agents who are willing to carry out people's wishes (i.e., public servants). This interpretation of the Golden Rule at the level of sovereignty highlights

---

[33] For verification, readers may refer to the placement of NG, PG, and NP in Figure 8a.

that the true locus of control for the rights enjoyed by the people are the people themselves, not the state or the government.

Let us now look at negative rights in more detail. As shown in Figure 12a, apart from acknowledging hard-to-pigeonhole things like Right to Life, the model automatically includes within it the concept of community rights, provided the individual gives active consent to such rights.[34] This is shown via the intersection area of the two circles in Figure 12a.

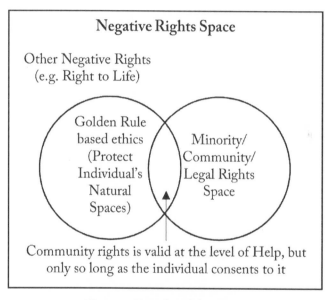

Fig-12a—Negative Rights Space

If there are community or minority rights where active consent of the individual is not possible or relevant, those rights can only become valid at the legal level of the model—the workings of which are captured in

---

[34] In this connection, it might be relevant to note what Eleanor Roosevelt said about being an individual: *"It is a brave thing to have courage to be an individual; it is also, perhaps, a lonely thing. But it is better than not being an individual, which is to be nobody at all."*

the later consolidation part of the model. Of course, these rights should not contradict the sanctity of individual liberty or its associated Complementary Rights. An example of this kind of community right might be the right to preserve the use of a regional language, regarding things like public notifications from the government.

Next, we examine positive rights. As shown in Figure 12b, top-down welfare delivery is represented by the right circle, and the bottom-up service delivery is represented by the left circle. Although neither the bottom-up service nor the top-down mandate is *justiciable* on its own, when they are taken together (i.e., the intersection space), they create a new space of positive rights that is indeed justiciable.

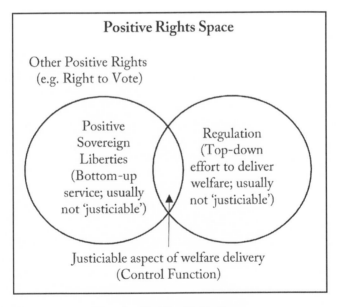

Fig-12b—Positive Rights Space

This should not be a surprise, for agreements need consent of both parties. In particular, to be seen as justiciable, the parameters must be directly related to both the bottom-up service rendered by individual agents and the top-down mandate of the people.[35]

As mentioned in Figure 12b, it is this justiciable, positive-rights space that is ensured by the Control-function. Moreover, since transparency is essential to all justiciable services, it must also be present. This is why rule-of-transparency was used to characterize the Control-function space in the previous chapter (refer to Figure 8a).[36]

Control-Function

Control-function is dealt with in this chapter, instead of in the earlier chapters, so as to avoid confusion regarding the nature of positive rights that are enabled by the model. After all, as shown in Figure 12b, since Control-function deals with only *justiciable* positive rights, this does not cover the full gamut of positive rights that may exist or can be enacted into law by governments.

Also, although the justiciable service angle is primarily a Stage-II responsibility, Control-function has additional responsibilities that

---

[35] Just as the rationale behind positive rights in the model is whether it is justiciable, the rationale behind negative rights is individual rights. Actually, the two criteria are present in both forms of rights. It is just that negative rights are easier to understand through the individuality prism, and positive rights in the model are easier to understand through the justiciable prism. Indeed, it is worth taking a moment to highlight the nature of change that occurs in the understanding of human rights when it is understood as justiciable and individual-based, rather than as non-justiciable and collective-based. For instance, positive rights in the model refer mainly to people's freedom to serve other people, and it exists because it is exercised voluntarily by people in their individual capacity. In contrast, the traditional understanding of positive rights refers only to actions that are to be done on behalf of citizens by the government, which is neither justiciable nor does it allow for a clearly discernable individual agency.

[36] We are not talking here of ensuring transparency in the functioning of public servants. While that might also be desirable in some situations, it would have to be justified on different grounds.

become relevant at Stage-III. For instance, at Stage-III level, Control-function probably should have the additional responsibility of calling out corruption at the Stage-II regulatory level.

Let us look at the responsibilities of the Control-function at Stage-II and Stage-III separately.

Stage-II Control-Function

Public servants must satisfy some minimum performance parameters with regard to their job profile. In particular, it is assumed that this should include at least three parameters:

1. Cost put on the people
2. Quality of their service capacity
3. Absence of any conflict of interest that could adversely affect their work

While the first two parameters may be referred to as *Cost* and *Quality*, the third parameter may be termed *Honesty*. For the sake of convenience, these three parameters can be referred to as the CHQ factors.

Incidentally, if we say each Control-function parameter must be made justiciable, it may not be easy to come up with parameters that are substantially different from the CHQ factors. Of course, researchers should take care to explore all the promising possibilities, as the results would only improve the model.

Notably, the presence of the three factors probably translates into a need for their corresponding regulatory functions, namely these: Audit, Recruitment/Retention, and Ombudsman. There is also a strong case to be made that these three Control-functions need to be kept independent of one another.[37] A brief overview of the three areas is given in Table 4.1.

While the Cost factor is mostly self-explanatory from the table, the other two factors probably require more explanation.

Table 4.1 Stage-II Control-Function's Regulation of Public Servants		
Factors	Functional Area	Relevant Parameters
Cost	Personnel Cost/Audit	Salaries and accountable perks of public servants
Quality	Personnel Quality	Recruitment (Exams), Retention (No passive bias)
Honesty	Personnel Ombudsman	Active conflict of interest among public servants

With regard to the Quality factor, Control-function is responsible for regulating the recruitment and retention of the personnel who want to serve the public. However, the *quality of work done* depends at least partly on the discretionary elements set in motion by the Executive, and therefore, regulating that aspect may not rest entirely with the Control-function. That being said, if some new passive characteristic, which carries the potential for future bias, has entered the profile of personnel who were earlier on the record as neutral, only the Control-function has the power to terminate the services of the personnel. Recruitment is done based on a minimum expectation of quality, and when the personnel breaks that agreement, action has to be taken.

---

[37] Of course, the requirement that the immunity-regulators be kept independent of the power-regulators is stronger, as is the need to separate the two immunity-regulators (Judiciary and Control-function) from each other. Fortunately, since these two latter requirements are clearly present in the model's structure, they scarcely need an additional emphasis.

For instance, affinity to particular political parties should probably be disallowed when it comes to public servants. A second flag could be the sudden appearance of large wealth in the public servant's family, with no known legal source. Yet another flag of passive bias could be the crossing of some key threshold, say in terms of absence from work or number of complaints from ordinary citizens who have interacted with the concerned public servant.

With regard to the Honesty factor, Control-function is responsible for minimizing active conflict of interest issues through the Ombudsman processes.[38] Corruption would be the most obvious manifestation of this problem. Another source could be a bias for or against members of a particular community, but this would have to be evidenced by some flagrant acts.

Although the Ombudsman also has the power to terminate the services of public servants, there is a big difference between terminating the services of a public servant via the Quality and Ombudsman processes. While the Quality process can only terminate services based on passive characteristics that have entered the profile of the public servant, Ombudsman can terminate based only on complaints received from the people regarding some activity.

Stage-III Control-Function

There is a big difference between the Control-function at the Stage-II and Stage-III levels. While the Stage-II Control regulation is directly over the public servants, the Stage-III level Control regulation is for maintaining the *transparent settings* of Stage-II regulators.

---

[38] Incidentally, Ombudsman is not just a European innovation. Countries like Botswana have also introduced successful approaches for dealing with corruption at the official level.

Therefore, it is possible that the Stage-III Control-function (Table 4.2) is better split into four distinct specializations corresponding to the four empowered-regulator types present at the Stage-II level. Clearly, this would be different from splitting the Control-function as per the three CHQ parameters, as done in Table 4.1. Nevertheless, since the pros and cons of the two approaches seem rather difficult to debate, the details of Control-function belonging to Table 4.2 are being presented in the same format as in Table 4.1. At the least, this makes it easy to compare the details of the Control-functions at the Stage-II and Stage-III levels.

Table 4.2 Stage-III Control-Function's Regulation of Empowered-Regulators		
Factors	Functional Area	Relevant Areas
Cost	Economy/Energy Audit	Audit of economy and energy supplies
Quality	Regulatory Quality	Election Commission, Judicial Commission, etc.
Honesty	Regulatory Ombudsman	Active conflict of interest among regulators

As part of the shift from Stage-II to Stage-III, which probably involves a more systematic bottom-up approach to the economy, it is necessary to have an independent accounting of economic performance and associated energy supplies.[39] This need is filled by the Audit function of Table 4.2.

The remaining two functions are simpler. The Recruitment function can be mapped to the election procedures of Legislative representatives

---

[39] It may appear odd that the *cost* factor maps onto the energy supplies that can be made available in the country, rather than something more tangible like the regulator salaries. However, at the Stage-III level, the more appropriate comparison may be the *energy supplies that can be made available*, since that is the final metric behind any cost. Also, the cost arising from regulator salaries is almost negligible when compared to the far larger cost arising from public servant salaries. Therefore, there may be a need to shift from a top-down understanding of *bureaucratic* cost to a bottom-up understanding of *system's delivery capacity*.

and the selection procedures of the other three regulatory officials (Judiciary, Executive, and Control). Similarly, the Ombudsman function can
be mapped to any specific instance of conflict of interest pertaining to
all these regulatory officials.

However, unlike the Stage-II Control-function, neither the Recruit-
ment-function nor the Ombudsman-function should have the power of
removal over the regulatory functionaries. As mentioned earlier, they are
limited to regulating the *transparent settings* of these regulators. If there
is to be a removal of regulatory officials from empowered-regulators, it
must be dealt with in a different manner than the removal of Stage-II
public servants.

For instance, there is the option of leaving the removal decision to
the other side, which lets the Legislature decide on immunity-regulators
and lets the Judiciary decide on power-regulators. Alternatively, there
could be a dedicated court in the Judiciary that would hear all the cases
brought forward by the Stage-III Control-function. Of course, this court
could also hear cases from public servants who feel they have been wrongly
terminated by the Stage-II Control-function.

Out of the two options, the dedicated-court option may make more sense
since we are attempting to enforce the rule of law here. Besides, the Legislature is not a suitable forum for deciding micro-level issues, like the
removal of regulatory officials, unless the official holds the highest office.

Remaining Stage-III Regulators

Since we have covered the Stage-III Control-function, let us look at the
other Stage-III regulators. Figure 8b highlights all four Stage-III regulators
by placing them inside the ovals. The diagram is meant to show that just
as there is a difference between the Stage-II and Stage-III Control-functions,

there are differences between the Stage-II and Stage-III manifestations of the remaining three regulators as well. The distinct-line patterns used to characterize the four empowered-regulators have already been used in Figure 8a. Here, the implied connection between each unshaded sovereign space and its adjacent shaded regulatory spaces is extended to the respective Stage-III regulators in the ovals.

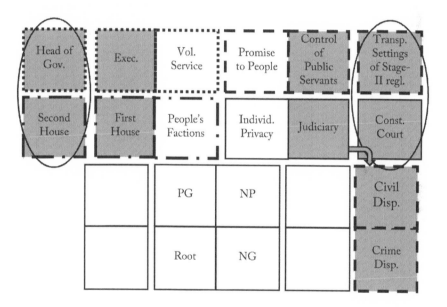

Fig-8b—Stage-III regulators are within the two ovals

We may summarize the situation with the other three Stage-III regulators as follows. The Stage-II Legislature, which can be unicameral, necessarily becomes bicameral at Stage-III; the Stage-II Judiciary, which looks at dispute resolutions, becomes the protector of Constitution at Stage-III; and the Stage-II Executive, which carries out the unavoidable discretionary activities, becomes directly responsible to the democratically elected head of government at Stage-III.

While the four Stage-III regulators can certainly be thought of as Stage-III empowered-regulators, they probably should not be thought of as unification-regulators. After all, it is the more complicated structure of Bicameral Legislature and the Supreme Court that forms the unification-regulators.

C. Individual–Group Rights

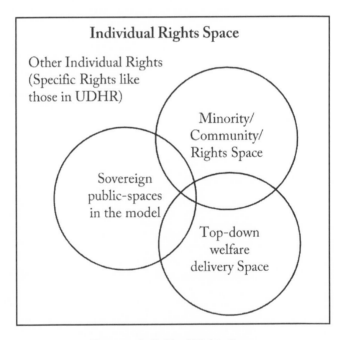

Fig-13a—Individual Rights Space

When it comes to Individual–Group Rights distinction, let us look at individual rights first. Obviously, individual rights should contain not only the negative and positive rights spaces, but also all the other spaces belonging to the sovereignty level. Thus, the circles of Figure 13a represent the details of not only Figure 12a (negative rights) and Figure 12b (positive rights), but also all the sovereign spaces. To be clear about this, the *minority/ community rights* circle is from Figure 12a; the *top-down welfare delivery space* is from Figure 12b; and the last circle represents the sovereign spaces in the model. In addition to these three broad categories, individual rights may also contain other items that can be specified by documents like the UDHR.

Next, let us investigate the domain of group rights. Traditionally, group rights might be seen as being present in the following four areas:

1. Commercial organizations (corporations, nonprofits, educational institutions, etc.)
2. Stakeholders of commercial organizations (shareholders, employees, customers, etc.)
3. Groups of commercial organizations (trade associations, chambers of commerce, etc.)
4. Non-commercial organizations (political parties, cultural organizations, religious orders, etc.)

However, despite there being at least four distinct types of groups that might want some sort of rights for themselves, only those groups falling within the first type of *commercial organizations* are directly accepted into the model's core structure.[40] Notably, the *commercial organization* is important enough to be treated as the principal building block present in the developmental extension (refer to Figure 6). The other three types of groups have to be handled in a more indirect manner by the model.

---

[40] For instance, including the noncommercial organizations here may subject the personal space of people (e.g., religious orders) to the discipline of a Constitutional structure, which is unacceptable.

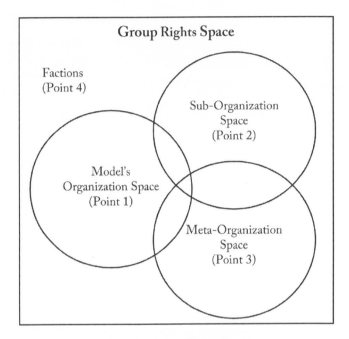

Fig-13b—Group Rights Space

Indeed, unlike negative and positive rights, which can be recognized almost immediately as subsets of the Sovereignty-Right, acknowledging the various group rights is a more complicated task. It certainly helps that group rights can be classified as operating at the sub-organization level, since that classification takes care of the second point in the previous list. Similarly, classifying group rights as operating at the meta-organization level takes care of the third point in the list. Therefore, we can plot the four traditional types of group rights as shown in Figure 13b, where the three circles are represented by the first three points in the list. The fourth point is present in the space outside the three circles.

With regard to the second point in the list, namely the sub-organizational space, stakeholders within commercial organizations can be given some rights at the legal level. This could be for employees, customers, shareholders, or citizens who want to bargain collectively against a larger entity like the commercial organization. Although the interests of the four stakeholders are represented at the level of the board, it is still possible that some specific rights cannot be directly given by the model. Therefore, they can be facilitated into existence at the legal level, in a manner similar to the minority and welfare rights discussed earlier.

With regard to the third point in the list, namely the meta-organizational space, although some legal rights can be given there, it is bound to be the source of a lot of organizational lobbying. Since monetary lobbying by organizations will be disproportionally influential in relation to lobbying by individuals, it can adversely affect the interests of the people. Consequently, governments must discourage the activity. Unlike the private space, the economic space is accessible to governments, and therefore, they can set some rules there.

Discussion on Factions

Regarding the fourth point in the list, it is rather different from the other three. It seems to have nothing to do with the organizational spaces in the model, and thus, it cannot be understood by looking at organizations in the developmental extension of the model. Instead, as far as this work is concerned, it might simply be understood as factions.

Madison offers a reasonably accurate take on these factions: *"By a faction, I understand a number of citizens whether amounting to a majority or a minority of the whole, who are united and actuated by some common impulse of passion, or of interest, adversed to the rights of citizens, or to the permanent and aggregate interests of the community."* Not just that, he goes on to say, *"Liberty is to faction, what air is to fire."*[41] If so, it seems to suggest that factions will be strengthened rather than weakened in the Constitutional setup, since the overriding goal in such systems is to expand and protect liberty.

The motivations of these factions are sourced directly from the private space of the people, where governments cannot enter. It is because of this powerful source base that these types of organizations can sustain and thrive, despite not being commercial with regard to their *raison d'*être. Factions are inevitably active at the final level of people's feedback. Consequently, they probably cannot be fully controlled by the regulations thought up by the Legislature.[42]

However, some indirect control can be exerted via meta-election rules, like the Bicameral setting, which leads to the process of competitive consensus formation at the feedback level. This process of consensus formation can be an indirect check on the power of a single faction since factions get to exercise their power only by cooperating with other factions, which can lead to a more moderate approach than any one dominant faction acting alone.[43] Another approach is via federations, where it is hoped that factions in each constituent state will behave in a relatively independent manner from those present in the other states.

---

[41] Incidentally, both of the Madison quotes are from the same essay, *Federalist*, no. 10.

[42] In fact, it is the other way around. Legislatures tend to be controlled by coalitions of these private-space factions.

[43] If we take this argument still further, Bicameral Legislature and Supreme Court, when they are taken together, have the ability to counterbalance the pressure from private-space factions of the Legislature. This ability can be achieved by democracies at Stage-III and will be shown in Figure 18.

D. Natural–Legal Rights

The Natural–Legal distinction in Rights theory is largely meant as a distinction between natural law and man-made law. Consequently, as far as comparing that distinction with the model's spaces is concerned, it is not going to be of much use. Natural law alone would take up all the spaces within the model, with the man-made law being restricted to just dealing with the output emerging from the Enactment-Right. This is shown in Figure 14a, with natural-rights space occupying all the space in the box on the right, while legal-rights space occupies just the smallest part of the box on the left.

Since comparing the model with Natural–Legal Rights distinction is not going to be useful, it is necessary to switch to a slightly different distinction in Rights theory, that of Moral–Legal, to get a better comparison with the model.

The model has been built using the Golden Rules, and therefore, the initial expansion part of the model conveys the main thrust on *morality* in that space. Moreover, as already noted in the build-up of the model, the Rights in the later consolidation part of the model have *legal* attributes and thus can be considered as legal rights.

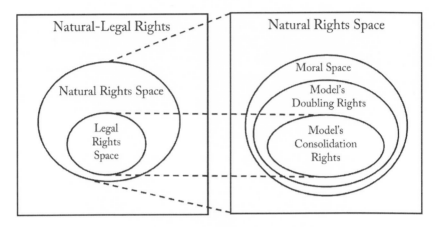

Fig-14a—Natural–Legal Rights distinction delineated
in terms of the Model's Spaces

As a result, the model can be thought of as adequately aligned with regard to the Moral–Legal Rights distinction since the two areas map directly to the two patterns in the model—namely initial expansion and later consolidation of the model. At the least, this alignment can be considered as more descriptive of the model than the original Natural–Legal Rights distinction we started with.

This later understanding is depicted on the right side of Figure 14a. Since the use of Golden Rules alone may not be enough to capture the full *Moral Space*, *Model's Doubling Rights* is shown as a subset of the larger *Moral Space*. On the other hand, *Model's Consolidation Rights* align with the *Legal Rights* shown in the box on the left.

Discussion on Medical and Biological Rights

Figure 14a cannot be considered as giving a complete picture unless it captures the *biological* angle conveyed by the term *natural*, since that is the meaning used in this work, prior to the discussion of Natural–Legal Rights.

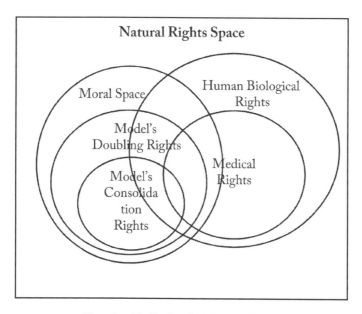

Fig-14b—Medical and Biological Rights

The biological aspect can perhaps be brought in from the founder of modern nursing, Florence Nightingale, and her words about nature's innate capacity to cure people: *"It is often thought that medicine is the curative process. It is no such thing...nature alone cures. Surgery removes the bullet out of the limb, which is an obstruction to cure, but nature heals the wound. So it is with medicine...And what nursing has to do in either case, is to put the patient in the best condition for nature to act upon him."*[44]

Nightingale seems confident in her assertion that nature alone ought to be trusted to cure living beings, at least at the levels below the

---

[44] The *nature* referred to by Nightingale is within the domains of biology. Therefore, for the things above the biological domain, nature cannot be guaranteed to cure. Taking corrective action at these higher levels probably requires deliberate human action. It is largely this space of deliberate human action that is represented by the Moral–Legal distinction shown in Figure 14a. Since the biological aspect is not modeled in that space, the biological angle has to be introduced separately in Figure 14b.

threshold of natural human capacity to intervene. In other words, human beings should not intervene at the level below where their natural access ends, lest the patient's health suffer as a consequence. Obviously, this is not a blanket ban. It merely means that all interventions at the lower level, especially if performed on humans, will have to pass some sort of medical assessment with regard to the potential for causing unintentional harm.

While the initial position of not interfering below a certain level could be termed *biological rights*, the more evolved position accepted by medical science as a matter of practice ought to be termed as the *medical rights* of the patient. Arguably, biological rights are similar to, but not the same as, the right for security of a person and the right against torture. On the other hand, the concept of medical rights is probably not yet explicitly enshrined in the UDHR paradigm.

This additional protection for all human beings that can be achieved through biological and medical rights is sought to be represented in Figure 14b by the two roughly concentric circles on the right side of the diagram.

2. RECONCILING MODEL WITH EXISTING PARADIGMS

In this second section of the chapter, we look to reconcile the model with the existing practice of human rights and democracies. After all, since this model has been created to improve the practice of human rights in democracies, it is necessary to reconcile it with the practical domain. First, we reconcile the Rights model with the existing approach of human rights. Next, we reconcile with the control exerted by private space values over democratic norms.

A. Model and the Existing Paradigm of Human Rights

The Rights model must be reconciled with the existing paradigm of human rights, as the current paradigm is obviously far more critical to the health of democracies than any theoretical proposal.

To start with, it is the first three Complementary Rights that capture the area traditionally understood as human rights. However, unlike the established human rights paradigm, which treats all rights as equally important, this model suggests a rough priority in the Complementary Rights, which essentially corresponds to their order of appearance in the model. Thus, the priority sequence of the Complementary Rights in the model would be of this form: Claim > Help > Sovereignty > Remaining Rights.

However, this should not be a surprising position, as what it implies is basically three uncontroversial distinctions:

1. Criminal disputes are more important than civil disputes
2. Protecting the private space is more important than developing the public space
3. People's sovereignty space is more important than the later regulatory spaces

To understand what violations of human rights could imply in practice, some egregious examples of human-rights abuse are examined below. First, with regard to the Claim-Right, starvation deaths, or even plain malnourishment of children, is a striking example. The numbers are mind-numbing at about several million every year. Another clear case of Claim-Right violation would be the problem of slavery, which is unfortunately still an issue affecting millions of lives across the world.

Second, with regard to Help-Right, anything that can be termed as a violation of parental freedom probably involves the Help-Right being restricted or violated in some manner. Examples of this could include the restraints placed on the Uyghur minority community's parenting rights in China's Xinjiang province,[45] or more generally, any unethical interference in family or parental activities. Third, with regard to Sovereignty-Right, a violation could involve the withholding of people's rights to assemble and decide their fate.[46]

Most violations of human rights, like in the Help-Right and Sovereignty-Right areas, involve multiple aspects of the theory, especially some aspect of the earlier Claim-Right. Indeed, most of these violations cannot be conveniently pigeonholed. Therefore, it makes sense to treat all rights as being equally important, so that all violations are addressed with sufficient priority.

Moreover, other than providing a useful analytical framework, it is not clear whether there are any inherent advantages to a priority order, since the final decision on rights must anyway be made only as per legally

---

[45] For instance, there are restrictions on naming of children and on religious fasts undertaken by minor-age students. Moreover, government-sponsored *reeducation* in Xinjiang is invading the private space (family life) of several million citizens. It appears designed to brainwash people into following the public line in their private lives. Recently, more disturbing reports have emerged which make it clear that the participation in some reeducation camps is forced on the people; it is not undertaken in a voluntary manner. If so, these camps would be a clear case of Claim-Right violation.

[46] If a region with territorial integrity has an independent Judiciary and free elections, it would be hard to make the case of a sovereignty violation. However, if certain sections of people are deliberately kept out of the public service cadre despite meeting objective, merit-oriented qualification criteria, that may also constitute a violation of sovereignty.

enforceable UDHR-like norms.[47] Thus, even though there are some truly distressing instances of Claim-Right violations that deserve more attention than they typically get from the world, the basic underlying approach of equal priority in the human rights paradigm is probably necessary to get justice to all whose rights are violated.[48]

Also, it is crucial to emphasize that the Rights model is meant for addressing governance failures, rather than changing the existing paradigm of human rights. For instance, several million people have had to flee Venezuela in the last few years. The motivation for this exodus may not be all that different from the refugees fleeing some Sub-Saharan countries. The cause is perhaps a failure of effective governance rather than outright human rights abuses at the level of the first three Rights.

These governance issues are correlated with the *Remaining Rights* in the model, which is an area largely glossed over by the existing human-rights paradigm. For instance, although the existing paradigm explicitly includes things like the right to vote, the actual working of the legal and regulatory spaces are only implicitly addressed as of now.

---

[47] However, there may be two areas where the priority ordering suggested by the model cannot be ignored in the practical or legal sense. The first one is the rights space of children, for they are not yet in a position where they can help adults in a meaningful manner. Therefore, their rights space is necessarily restricted to the Life and Claim-Rights alone, at least as per the adult framing that runs the world. For instance, a legal contract entered into by a person of a minor age is probably not enforceable. Similarly, in the case of crimes against noncitizens within a country, only the first two Rights are implicated. Noncitizens do not have access to the third Sovereignty-Right. Fortunately, having access to the first two Rights implies the private space of noncitizens is just as sacrosanct as that of normal citizens.

[48] As of now, the Remaining Rights, namely those that come after the Sovereignty-Right, would tend to be violated, even if only in some minor way, across most countries. Therefore, it may be true that at a default level, the first three Rights are considered more important than the rest. Moreover, although violations of the first three Rights are specifically discussed here, particular violations of the Remaining Rights are not discussed here, for that list would be too long. Arguably, a good bit of the rest of this work is an attempt to discuss those issues in a relatively comprehensive manner.

It need not be so. The human rights paradigm can be clear about the details inherent in all legal workings without changing itself or compromising its integrity in any way.

B. Private Space Human Values Control Democracies

Human and community values form a powerful factor in people's lives and tend to make their presence felt via people's feedback in democracies. Since it was argued in the first chapter that the final Feedback-Right integrates into the whole model, especially at the level of the sovereignty spaces, closer examination is required to pin down the real source of human values within the model's spaces. Keep in mind, this more granular understanding of the private space in the model is exploratory and definitely not part of the model's theory.

Since Claim-Right is mandatory for all individuals regardless of people's unique value systems, it probably cannot be the source of any differential influence in democracies. Instead, idiosyncratic human values would have to be viewed as active at the level of the root element.

At the level of the Help-Right (refer to Figure 2), the left space can perhaps be thought of as reflecting community norms of helping others (e.g., use of a language). On the other hand, the space on the right can be thought of as representing family or community values. People generally prefer to marry those who hold belief and value convictions similar to their own, perhaps because it reduces the potential for conflicts in the upbringing of children.

Also, private behavior can be modeled only so far as it has a bearing on the public behavior, and no more than that. This is one of the reasons why this particular model cannot be made to contain all the various human rights present in the UDHR. Therefore, the model cannot ever hope to replace the UDHR. For instance, rights which would need to be handled on subjective humanistic terms would include things like religion, language, and custom. Clearly, a model that is focused on a non-contradictory, logical structure does not have the capacity to pin down aspects of human values like that.

In summary, it is quite likely that without the helping hand provided by human values, governments would not be in a position to increase people's liberty space. In other words, it is the private space human values, which cannot be made part of a public space model, that contribute to the core foundation for democracies to thrive in nations.[49]

---

[49] As far as Stage-II is concerned, it is mostly the feudal governance structures (*extractive institutions* of Acemoglu and Robinson) that hold them back from moving to the democratic Stage-III. In other words, Stage-II nations are mostly stuck at their level because of their elites and not solely because of their people's private space values. Moreover, although *Why Nations Fail* rejects the role played by environmental settings (it accepts the role played by contingencies of history), this work will argue that the environment plays a big role in shaping the norms of societies.

4

Avoidable
Misinterpretations

The possibility of misinterpretations is especially relevant when the topic is as broad as the Constitutional structure. Consequently, great care needs to be taken to clarify areas within the model that might be susceptible to misinterpretations.

As we shall see, a good deal of effort has been devoted in this direction. There are three sections in this chapter, with the first section focused on the misinterpretations related to the first two chapters; the second section focused on the third chapter; and the last section focused on issues related to how the model may interact with the surrounding environment.

Obviously, not all possible misinterpretations can be addressed here, for that list might well be infinite. Only the areas that are most likely to be misunderstood can be included. In addition, it may be a good practice to restrict this kind of discussion to a length that is shorter than the main work. If it exceeds the size of the main work, then perhaps the main work itself should be made larger, so that more of the reader's attention is devoted in that direction.

Also, since it is imperative that the misinterpretation areas be understood with as little effort as possible, each area is phrased as "attempting to force-fit something with respect to the model." Needless to say, in each such case, the position of this work is that the model cannot be made to imply that "something" without destroying it altogether.

1. MISINTERPRETATIONS RELATED TO THE FIRST TWO CHAPTERS

Some of the more notable misinterpretation possibilities related to the first two chapters are as follows:

1. Force-fitting the model as an alternative to UDHR-like norms
2. Force-fitting the model's practical applicability as capable of becoming fully logical
3. Force-fitting the model as capturing the entire space of morality
4. Force-fitting the model as assuming that human nature is bad
5. Force-fitting the model as capable of implying the decisions of the Supreme Court
6. Force-fitting the Judiciary's powers as being equal to that of the Legislature
7. Force-fitting organizational privacy as equally sacrosanct as individual privacy
8. Force-fitting organizations as having the same freedom as individuals to lobby in the democratic space

Attempting to Force-Fit the Model as an
Alternative to UDHR-Like Norms

This model is intended only as an aid for better analysis so that rights violations in the public spaces can be prevented. It is certainly not intended as an alternative to the established paradigm of human rights, which is understood to be largely represented by the UDHR.

Consequently, it should be understood that if there are any areas of ambiguity between the model and UDHR, then UDHR should prevail.[50] Although UDHR-like rights may not be as logically sound as the model, that is not a flaw, for the domain of humanities in which they operate is such that some seeming contradictions might be allowed to coexist, if that is necessary to maintain peace.

Thus, the core idea is to retain the established paradigm of making human rights decisions via norms like UDHR, while introducing the possibility for new analytical tools, which could potentially increase the accuracy of public-space decisions made within that paradigm. If this particular model is not good enough, then perhaps some other model that agrees on the core premise of human rights and liberty might prove adequate for the job.

For instance, if the selected model could increase the accuracy in human rights decisions with regard to the public spaces, from about 90 percent to 95 percent, it would have fulfilled its expectations. However, most of that improvement may not accrue immediately and might

---

[50] For instance, the concept of negative and positive rights might seem to be possible areas of contention. Fortunately, these are dealt with in Figure 12a and Figure 12b.

take several generations of careful study.[51] Even in a situation where the model is almost completely understood, it still does not make sense to seek anything beyond an incremental improvement of the sort imagined above. This is because we are quite clear about remaining firmly within the established human rights paradigm of UDHR-like norms.[52]

It should also be clarified that the model seeks to improve human rights in only certain delimited areas. In particular, analyzing activities in people's private space is mostly out of bounds for it. That is the area where UDHR-like norms will always be required. For example, the freedom to make formal contracts in the private space, like in the case of marriages or partnerships, cannot be constrained by this model. Instead, the model is appropriate only for analyzing activities in the public space of sovereignty and governance. Indeed, it has many suggestions in that space.

Moreover, even though some additional clarity is created in the public space by the model, it still stays within the paradigm created by UDHR. As an example, Article 21 of UDHR contains the right to vote. Since that Article assumes the existence of democracies, arguably there is an underlying need for models on the functioning of democracies.

---

[51] Moreover, it is advisable to be skeptical of models which promise far more improvement than something like the 5 percent mark, because that runs the risk of disagreeing with Arendt's position on nonviolence. At a minimum, the improvement must take care to capture the essential details of the existing paradigm. In other words, society should not be too open when it comes to improvements rejecting the established paradigms, for that kind of unrestrained openness could easily lead to collapse.

[52] This should not be taken to mean UDHR is perfect or that it cannot be improved. Obviously, it can be improved. For instance, the coming discussion of genomic and neural sciences (in Chapter Five) suggests the coverage of UDHR should be extended to those areas. But the process for that improvement will have to be based on international cooperation. An analytical work on rights, which by definition cannot operate at that level, must take care to remain within the bounds set by the international norms, provided those norms have been improving the lot of human welfare.

Attempting to Force-Fit the Model's Practical Applicability
as Capable of Becoming Fully Logical

Since the model aims to provide analytical clarity, it aims to be logical as far as possible. However, no theoretical model's applicability to the practical human world is ever capable of becoming fully logical. If that is to happen, it would require the human world to become fully logical, completely divorced from human concerns and fears, which is impossible.

Besides, since the model is clearly restricted to operating as an analytical aid within the larger paradigm created by UDHR, it already means that the model's practical applicability cannot be made fully logical. After all, the UDHR paradigm would not allow it.

The overall lesson here is that it would be wrong to expect a logical model to have anywhere near the necessary power to convey all the complexities inherent in the human world of values. Logical clarity in the model is desirable only to the extent it can aid in its analytical utility. Taking it further than that will eventually destroy the model's applicability for the human world. Of course, the drawback to any model's lack of logical rigor is that it could be misinterpreted.

Attempting to Force-Fit the Model as Capturing
the Entire Space of Morality

The model uses the negative and positive versions of the Golden Rule to map out a set of spaces, which is described as representing the concept of *morality* (refer to Figure 5). However, it is crucial to acknowledge that *morality* is a much larger concept than the narrow set of spaces mapped within the model.

This can be appreciated by looking at the concept of *altruistic* morality as being slightly different from the concept of *reciprocal* morality. While the morality space within the model is arguably limited to the understanding of the reciprocal principle present within the Golden Rule, altruistic morality will aim to help people without expecting anything at all in return. Altruistic morality is probably the type of morality that is encouraged as the ideal to aspire to in spiritual traditions like religions.

However, when people are wronged in some manner, and appeal to the judicial system for relief from their tormentors, the expectation is probably for an adjudication based on the principle of fairness, which requires a reciprocal understanding of the situation. If the adjudication is instead based on altruism, people will no longer have a firm control over the direction or the product of their labors. Therefore, this model is necessarily based on reciprocal morality.

However, it needs to be made clear that the model also allows for other larger ideas of morality to flourish in the private space of people. Perhaps it can be argued that a model based on the reciprocal principle is likely to facilitate much more liberty for all individuals, so that even the liberty space for pursuing altruistic morality gets dramatically enhanced.

Attempting to Force-Fit the Model as Assuming That Human Nature Is Bad

Since the negative version of the Golden Rule is invoked prior to the positive version, it might lead people to misunderstand the model's position. People might think that the model necessarily assumes human nature is bad. That would be a grossly incorrect extrapolation from the model.

The reason the negative version of the Golden Rule is placed first is because the pro-social voluntary activities would shrink or collapse if they are forced to coexist in an environment where human generosity is systematically exploited by the few bad agents that exist in society. The model assumes that once these bad agents no longer have a free run, people's natural preference for good behavior will shine through. In other words, the model implicitly assumes human nature is mostly good, for the simple reason that the model is almost entirely based on people's voluntary proclivities.

Indeed, the assumption that human nature is good is not just an empty theoretical supposition. We can verify it empirically. For instance, if too much effort must necessarily be deployed by developed country governments toward the enforcement of the negative Golden Rule, it can perhaps be argued that human nature is bad. Fortunately, data tells us this is definitely not the case. The percentage of people who undertake activities that could be deemed criminal or illegal does not ever seem to rise to even a low figure like 5 percent. Actually, it probably does not reach even half that number.

Incidentally, according to early Chinese philosopher Mencius, "*Human nature is inherently good, just like water flows inherently downhill.*"[53] This work thinks that the above analogy is correct in almost all instances. Moreover, even in the few cases where things go wrong, perhaps due to unfortunate circumstances, it is quite possible that better guidance and coaching would enable the concerned people to mend their ways. Admittedly, it should also be noted here that modern psychological studies suggest that a certain percentage of people have shortcomings that would be hard to ameliorate. Fortunately, as discussed in the above paragraph, that

---

[53] The translation is by David Hinton.

percentage is so low that a well-functioning society can easily handle the complications.

Attempting to Force-Fit the Model as Capable of Implying the Decisions of the Supreme Court

If the decisions of the Supreme Court are to be understood, they must be analyzed with regard to the context and all the associated details, which this work cannot do. This model, or for that matter any other model, cannot reach anywhere near the power to deal comprehensively with all the details that will be present in complex Court decisions. The most they can do is criticize or support some artificially isolated aspect of a decision.

In fact, even instances where such narrow positions become defendable are likely to be rare, for models can only defend something if it can be shown as emerging from within its own conceptual structure. However, all working Constitutions are full of practical positions that cannot be logically derived from conceptual models. Consequently, Constitutional positions are legal in nature and outside the domain of theoretical models.

This is one of the main reasons why this model cannot be made to imply the *basic structure* doctrine of the Indian Supreme Court, which resulted from the *Kesavananda Bharati* verdict. The Court's *basic structure* doctrine necessarily relies only on the assertions present, or implied, in a particular Constitutional document, whereas this model obviously cannot restrict itself to just one legal document. As a result, the conclusions that will be reached by the two approaches may differ in many areas (e.g., federal systems may not be a perfect fit for the model).

That said, if the *basic structure* doctrine is a correct position, it is likely that there will be a need for a logical model that holds at a more abstract level. However, this particular model need not be that deeper level structure. For all we know, there may be some other conceptual structures that are superior to it.

Attempting to Force-Fit Judiciary's Powers as Being Equal to That of the Legislature

There should be no doubt that Legislature is the most powerful regulator among the empowered-regulators, with the Judiciary coming second. It is important to clarify this point, since the high priority accorded to the protection of private space could get misinterpreted to mean that the Judiciary is more powerful, when that is definitely not the case.

Legislature is more powerful because it enjoys relative freedom to prioritize its actions, based on its perceptions of people's wishes. By contrast, Judiciary can only interpret the laws put in place by the Legislature, so as to avoid contradictions in them. This aspect is made even clearer when we consider the fact that Legislature regulates Hohfeld's *Power* of the people, while Judiciary regulates Hohfeld's *Immunity* of the people.

The only area where the Judiciary might mistakenly be thought of as superior to Legislature is with regard to the importance of its core function, as the need to protect the people's private space is thought to be more important than even the power of making new laws. However, even when it comes to protecting the fundamental privacy of citizens, it is the Legislature that frames the relevant laws.

Judiciary can only ensure that the privacy-related laws do not contradict Judiciary's *raison d'être*—the need for an institution that will defend the private space of the people from public spaces. If the private space can be violated by the public space, the public space will essentially invalidate its reason for existence, since it would have become adversarial as per the understanding of the model.

Moreover, while Legislature is more powerful than Judiciary, it does not owe its powerful position to an exclusive relationship with the people, for the Judiciary also represents the people's voice. It is just that, compared to the Judiciary, Legislature has relatively superior access to people in the public space. After all, judicial interactions with people must necessarily be done at arm's length to preserve its neutrality.

While Legislature is given its voice directly by the people's votes, Judiciary gets its voice from the people's best reasoning for avoiding contradictions. Needless to say, both the casting of votes and dispute resolutions are highly structured processes, and both should be done in a manner that most suits the people's needs. In the modern Constitutional democracies, these processes have evolved to a high degree of sophistication, keeping in mind people's needs in both arenas.

Finally, from the perspective of the model, while Legislature is the most powerful of the empowered-regulators, it is important to remember that there are three other regulators operating at the sovereignty level (not just the Judiciary). The structure of the model is such that it does not permit just one or two regulators to be present. There must be four regulators since the prior spaces in the model, which need to be regulated, require that. Therefore, while understanding the relative importance and functioning of any one of the four regulators, it is necessary to take into account the presence of the other three regulators and their respective functions.

Attempting to Force-Fit
Organizational Privacy as Being at the
Same Level as Individual Privacy

Although the concept of privacy applies both at the commercial-organization level and the individual level, the details in the two cases are quite different. Privacy at the individual level is sacrosanct and cannot be challenged. On the other hand, privacy at the commercial-organization level is just an artificial requirement that is extrapolated from the human commercial spaces. Since organizational space is an artificial construct, privacy in that space hinges on what people think will best aid them in the economic sphere.

As a consequence, it is likely that the optimum, organizational, privacy position cannot be completely theorized *a priori*. Instead, many bounds around organizational privacy will have to be discovered by well-thought-out actions, primarily from the Legislature and the Judiciary. For instance, in the case of serious fraud or systemic risks, board privacy may be suspended by the Judiciary, so that government can act to rectify the situation. Of course, these would be rare situations.

Attempting to Force-Fit
Organizational Lobbying as Being at the
Same Level as Individual Lobbying

Since there can be no question of treating organizations at par with human beings, it is necessary to curtail their freedom to lobby governments, especially by making donations. After all, they wield disproportional spending power with respect to the people. If organizations can lobby with the same freedom as people, it will probably lead to the cul-de-sac of corporate-rule.[54]

Nevertheless, it is probably also necessary to create regulated avenues where the opinions of organizations on regulations can be made transparently available to the public. As a consequence of such an arrangement, these opinions would automatically become available to regulators as well. In effect, this would require that all commercial organizations be legally prevented from having any undue relationship (e.g., monetary) with the people who lobby regulatory officials.

It should also be noted that lobbying freedom of normal organizations likely differs from infra-organizations. After all, since infra-organizations are comparable to public servants, not all information they share with the government can be made transparent (rule-of-transparency applies only for Control-function, not for public servants). However, if any transparency rules are made mandatory for the work done by public servants, some such rules could also be made to apply on the work done by infra-organizations.

2. MISINTERPRETATIONS RELATED TO CHAPTER THREE

Some of the more important misinterpretation possibilities related to Chapter Three can be listed as follows:

---

[54] In this connection, the US Supreme Court ruling in *Citizens United* might someday be compared to the mistake made in the *Dred Scott* case, which was an instance when the Court attempted to defend the dreadful practice of slavery. The two cases are striking examples of how some rare Supreme Court decisions violate the core structural principles underpinning the Rights theory of the Constitutional model.

1. Force-fitting the embodied understanding of negative Golden
   Rule as unimportant
2. Force-fitting the model as incapable of capturing the spaces
   implied by the four Rights distinctions
3. Force-fitting the model as wary of all negative *organization rights*,
   but welcoming all non-justiciable positive rights

Attempting to Force-Fit the Embodied Understanding
of Negative Golden Rule as Unimportant

The first Complementary Right in the model, the Claim-Right, must be
understood in an embodied or biological manner. Notably, this is somewhat different from the more objective understanding of law, which is
strived for in various statutes and associated judicial decisions. The distinction is relatively clear in Figure 9.

The legal approach has to be more objective because it has to be understood in a *standard* way. Otherwise, statutes and associated judicial decisions cannot be communicated without errors to all people. By contrast,
the embodied understanding of the Golden Rule comes from a person's
own conscience and requires no governmental enforcement.

It is quite critical to understand that the embodied view of the negative
Golden Rule is an integral part of the model. It is not possible to internalize
an objective version of the negative Golden Rule without accepting that
the original source of the negative Golden Rule is the embodied version.
For instance, if we pretend that the embodied biological version is not
important, and pay attention only to an objective version, it potentially
opens the door to totalitarian governments.

Attempting to Force-Fit the Model as
Not including the Spaces Implied
by the Rights Distinctions

The four Rights distinctions mentioned in Wikipedia's page on *Rights* was the key stepping-stone for the framing of this model.[55] Although it may initially appear as though the model does not directly imply all the possibilities implied in the Rights distinctions, in actual practice, the model does include the entire space implied by the Rights distinctions. This is due to the presence of its later consolidation part, which can create more human rights protections by the simple procedure of legal enactments or Constitutional amendments.

For instance, with regard to the traditional Claim–Liberty Rights, the model's Claim-Right seems to imply only the area represented by the negative Golden Rule. However, as shown in Figure 9, the space of all national laws is also acknowledged by the model, through the later consolidation part of the model. The story is similar with regard to Negative–Positive Rights and Individual–Group Rights as well, as shown in the set of figures from Figure 12a to Figure 13b.

Although new rights can be added onto the spaces identified in the above diagrams through legislations, these legislated rights protections perhaps cannot be improved by knowing the model's structure. The enacted rights will simply exist as legislated, provided the legislation does not violate basic liberty and private space norms.

---

[55] Wikipedia. "Rights." https://en.wikipedia.org/wiki/Rights (Last accessed on May 3, 2022).

Attempting to Force-Fit the Model as
Wary of All Negative Organization Rights, but Welcoming
of All Non-Justiciable (Legally Enacted) Positive Rights

It has already been explained that *organization rights* cannot be made a mandatory part of the model, primarily because the commercial organization is an artificial construct. However, this position should not be misconstrued to mean that *organization rights* are to be considered as altogether undesirable within the model. In fact, it is more desirable to have some form of negative *organization rights* that can be legitimately enforced by the courts, than it would be to create non-justiciable positive rights for citizens through legal enactments.

After all, anything that is not justiciable by the citizens is likely to lead to an abuse of governmental and bureaucratic power. Indeed, as per our current understanding, anything that is outside the CHQ schema automatically risks not being justiciable. It is, of course, worthwhile to have more debates about whether there can be new approaches, outside of the CHQ schema, for achieving justiciable services for citizens.

It is to be noted that the soft biological infrastructure areas like food, water, education, and healthcare can easily fit under the CHQ schema. It is more a question of whether the policy makers will respect the people's innate need for justiciable services, so that people can hold the service providers accountable for poor performance on some agreed-upon parameters. Indeed, justiciable services go beyond mere accountability since people can redress their grievances via complaints.

3. MISINTERPRETATIONS RELATED
TO THE ENVIRONMENT

Finally, we need to look at some misinterpretation possibilities related to the interaction of the model and the environment. Our understanding of the model would be gravely incomplete if it is viewed completely independent of the environment.

Here, the prominent misinterpretation possibilities are the following:

1. Force-fitting the model as a mandate for all systems to move to Stage-III level
2. Force-fitting the model as a mandate for all systems to move to Stage-IV level
3. Force-fitting the model as suggesting that Stage-IV systems are unnecessary

Attempting to Force-Fit the Model as a Mandate
for All Systems to Move to Stage-III Level

We have quoted Mencius earlier in this chapter: "*Human nature is inherently good, just like water flows inherently downhill.*" It is notable that Mencius uses the above-mentioned analogy of *water flowing downhill* in another way as well—to suggest that human nature prefers those governments that can keep their people clear of the things they hate and surround them with what they want.

However, unlike Mencius, who is theorizing strictly within a Stage-II system, this work is explicitly trying to achieve Stage-III systems. Therefore, it is not clear if the second water analogy, the one made in the context of governance, will hold for this work. For instance, the continuing existence of Stage-II systems strongly suggests that there are other factors at play as well. Indeed, it may be the case that achieving Stage-III systems is not determined purely by human nature.

Instead, it is possible that although human nature is good and naturally prefers governments that can reduce the bad things people face in life, various environmental challenges in some geographies are serious enough to prevent Stage-III norms being adopted in those regions.[56] In other words, as far as the water analogy goes, achieving Stage-III systems require special providential circumstances where the water can pool and then rise up.

This likely means the environmental factors exert a disproportional influence over people's value systems, and if those inimical environmental factors are to be overcome by human effort, at a minimum, it will require a world where Stage-IV systems hold sway for an unprecedented period of time.

Attempting to Force-Fit the Model as a Mandate for All Systems to Move to Stage-IV Level

To start with, the existence of commercial activities at the Stage-II level does not imply the existence of formal, commercial organizations like

---

[56] As already noted, another view is also possible on why achieving Stage-III is difficult, which is that extractive elites prevent the rise of inclusive institutions. It may be added here that this view of selfish elite behavior probably does not contradict the view held by Mencius, since his view is about the common people. As far as the elites are concerned, apart from the natural wish to protect their wealth, there is also the matter of group dynamics where the fact that many elites benefit from the system creates an entrenched behavior to protect the system.

those modeled as part of Stage-IV.[57] Instead, Stage-III is probably necessary to bring about that transformation. Stage-III can be thought of as
the intermediate stage where the agricultural surplus-based Stage-II can
potentially be transformed into Stage-IV, such that most of the Stage-IV
energy surplus is from nonagricultural sources.[58] However, the transformation to Stage-IV cannot be guaranteed, since it is quite possible
that the environmental situation may not be conducive enough for it to
be achieved.

Moreover, it is possible that in cases where there are no serious challenges from climate and environment, Stage-III alone might prove sufficient to achieve an adequate level of environmental stability, at least
for a short term. Hence, it might also be argued that there is no need for
Stage-IV systems in some situations.

It is because of this lack of certainty regarding the achievability and
desirability of Stage-IV that the model cannot treat Stage-IV as a must-
have stage across all possible circumstances. Instead, Stage-IV must be
treated as a desirable extension to the model that becomes possible only
when the conditions are conducive for it.

---

[57] It is relatively obvious that commercial activities of some sort must already exist at the level of Stage-II
(and even Stage-I) since trade and commerce are quite ingrained in human activities. In particular, even
something as sophisticated as public infrastructure would already be present at the Stage-II level. After
all, large amounts of food surplus cannot come into existence all by itself; it requires some governance
systems to be put in place, so that the surplus can be productively channeled into nonagricultural activities like handicrafts and trading.

[58] *Mala fide* disputes at Stage-II would be about charges of tax evasion at the level of individual citizens.
Although this would hold to an extent at Stage-III as well, it is *mala fide* behavior from public servants that
would be dealt with more seriously at Stage-III. Further, when it comes to Stage-IV, it can be argued that
an individual's tax evasion (if the concerned income is not from commercial organizations) should be
treated less seriously than tax evasion done by organizations. After all, commercial organizations cannot
exist without the nation, whereas people have no such existential dependence on the state.

Attempting to Force-Fit the Model as Suggesting
That Stage-IV Systems Are Unnecessary

It must be emphasized that the lack of certainty about the need and viability of Stage-IV can be resolved if the actual situation is known, for then
the practical feasibility of Stage-IV can be assessed. It is via this kind
of practical assessment that it becomes possible for us to estimate that
achieving Stage-IV systems is both possible and absolutely necessary in
the current context we live in. This is because without the technological
capacity and energy surplus made possible by Stage-IV systems, there is
likely to be massive human suffering in the future.[59]

Moreover, even though Stage-III systems might be able to achieve an
adequate amount of environmental stability in some situations, it implies
economic impoverishment of the people. From a longer-term perspective,
regardless of its environmental stability, Stage-III food production systems
almost certainly cannot achieve stability with respect to the climate. Making a nation's food supply secure from the vagaries of long-term climate
change is a task that will be challenging even at the Stage-IV level.

In order to understand the danger from climatic variations, we just
need to look at two historical temperature records, that of the last 12,000
years and that of the last 800,000 years. While the average temperature
stays in a narrow range of about one degree centigrade in the former,
it regularly fluctuates by more than ten degrees in the latter.[60] Clearly,
Earth's natural variation in temperature over a long enough period is

---

[59] For more information, please refer to well-known books by William R. Catton and Donella H. Meadows,
titled *Overshoot* and *Limits to Growth*, respectively.

[60] Wikipedia. "Global temperature record." https://en.wikipedia.org/wiki/Global_temperature_record
(Last accessed on May 3, 2022).

devastatingly variable from the viewpoint of settled human societies. Certainly, modern agriculture cannot survive under such variations. Thus, there should be no doubt that climate resilience is of grave existential importance.

Having said that, it is not necessary for all nations to achieve the Stage-IV level of development. From a strictly practical perspective, just a few nations achieving Stage-IV might get the crucial technological breakthroughs that are necessary. Other nations might be able to leverage the benefits made available by the Stage-IV technologies to manage their internal energy needs.

Part Two

PEOPLE'S EXPECTATIONS *from* SOCIETIES

5

People's Expectations from Sovereignty

Now that we have introduced the Constitutional structure and explained its theoretical background, we are in a position to examine people's expectations from democracies, at least as represented by Stage-III and Stage-IV of the model. However, before we look at democracies, we need to understand people's expectations from sovereignty itself. Accordingly, this chapter is meant to look at a few crucial aspects of sovereignty.

This chapter has two sections. First, a discussion on *working dynamics*, which looks at the internal workings of the sovereignty space. Second, a discussion on *lower limits*, which investigates the *minimum factors* that are necessary to ensure stability of the sovereign system.

1. WORKING DYNAMICS OF SOVEREIGNTY SPACE

The working dynamics of sovereignty within the model is examined in three parts. The first part lays out three distinct approaches for understanding liberty. The second part introduces *Sovereign-liberties*, which involves mapping the noted British political theorist Isaiah Berlin's analysis of liberty onto the sovereign spaces present in the model. The third part explains some of the dynamics associated with the abovementioned Sovereign-liberties.

A. Three Ways to Understand Liberty

The model's view on liberty can be understood from at least three distinct perspectives:

1. Mandela's freedoms
2. Berlin's liberties
3. Improvement-perspective

Mandela's freedoms can be understood from his quote on freedom given at the start of Chapter One: *"For to be free is not merely to cast off one's chains, but to live in a way that respects and enhances the freedom of others."* Since it clearly puts the focus on *respect the freedom of others* and *enhance the freedom of others*, it does not seem to require a further elaboration. By contrast, the next two perspectives require a close analysis.

The second perspective on liberty comes from Isaiah Berlin. His approach is to separate liberty into two different strands, namely negative and positive liberty. Berlin defines negative liberty as, *"What is the area within which the subject—a person or group of persons—is or should be left to do or be what he is able to do or be, without interference by other persons?"* By contrast, he defines positive liberty as, *"What, or who, is the source of control, or interference that can determine someone to do, or be, this rather than that?"*

Although both liberties are equally essential to human freedom, Berlin was more wary of positive liberty being misused to suppress negative liberty. Indeed, it is arguable that the above definitions contain this concern. Rather than having to read this whole work to get to a more balanced position on positive liberty, readers may simply refer to Mandela's quote to get a more balanced outlook. Mandela's *respect the freedom of others* is almost the same as Berlin's negative liberty, and Mandela's *enhance the freedom of others* possibly offers a more balanced view of positive liberty than Berlin's definition does.

The third perspective on liberty involves adopting an *improvement-perspective* toward liberty, which implies that gains in liberty should be actively sought. Notably, this improvement-perspective is different from the implicit perspective present in Berlin's analysis of liberties, for Berlin seems to adopt a *maintenance-perspective* toward liberty, which implies loss of liberty must be avoided.

The *improvement* filter leads to viewing liberty from the *normative* and *statutory* angles. The normative side is probably best understood in terms of the German enlightenment thinker Immanuel Kant's deontological outlook, which tends to ignore crucial existing realities. The statutory side is best understood in terms of the need to comply with currently existing laws, which tends to ignore the merit of those laws.

Crucially, just as Berlin's analysis of the two liberties reveals that they are complementary to each other, the normative and statutory sides of liberty are also complementary. For instance, since the normative-position (e.g., Kant's categorical imperatives)[61] assumes an ideal world

---

[61] Kant's deontological outlook, as represented by the categorical imperatives, is a notable example of this. Kant has proposed several formulations of the categorical imperative. For instance, "Act only according to that maxim whereby you can, at the same time, will that it should become a universal law," and, "Act in such a way that you treat humanity, whether in your own person or in the person of any other, never merely as a means to an end, but always at the same time as an end."

where everyone strives to be perfectly good, it needs the statutory-position of existing laws to punish the norm violators. By contrast, since the statutory-position (e.g., Montesquieu's position)[62] emphasizes compliance with the laws, it needs the normative-position if it is to improve itself over time.

Table 5.1 Different Approaches to Liberty		
Mandela's Freedoms	Respects freedom of others	Enhances freedom of others
Different Perspectives on Liberty		
Maintenance-perspective	Berlin's negative liberty	Berlin's positive liberty
Improvement-perspective	Statutory (Existing laws)	Normative (Kant's ethics)
Differences Recast in terms of *Agency*		
Top-down agency of government	Statutory (existing laws)	Berlin's positive liberty
Bottom-up agency of individuals	Berlin's negative liberty	Normative (Kant's ethics)

While the maintenance- and improvement-perspectives are clearly laid out as the second and third rows of Table 5.1, it is to be noted that the exact same contents are also laid out in the last two rows representing the top-down agency of the government and the bottom-up agency of the individual. The key difference is that in the latter case, where the placement is in terms of *agency*, the contents of maintenance- and improvement-perspectives are diagonally spread between the last two

---

[62] Montesquieu's position on liberty is an example of this: *"Liberty is the right of doing whatever the laws permit."*

rows, and not contained in a single row. Thus, the table shows that there is a basic equivalence between viewing liberty in terms of maintenance- and improvement-perspectives, when compared to viewing it in terms of top-down and bottom-up perspectives.

Moreover, once we see the layout of the liberties in terms of *agency*, it is clear that just as Berlin's negative liberty seems preferable to his positive liberty, the normative-position seems preferable to the statutory-position. The reason for this preference is the same in both cases—it is the bottom-up agency that is preferable to people.

Evidently, Berlin's preference for negative liberty is not a defect of the theory, but rather a result of the way in which the problem is approached. When the same problem is approached from the opposite side of the improvement-perspective, people's preference naturally shifts to positive liberty, since that is where the bottom-up agency of the individual shifts to. By contrast, Mandela's perspective on freedom gives the preferred bottom-up understanding of liberty on both sides of the equation because it is based entirely on the individual's own agency.

However, out of the three approaches, it is Berlin's definition of liberties that is the most adept when it comes to discussing the topic of this Constitutional model. Besides, it is also the most well-known position in academic circles.[63] Consequently, this work will rely on Berlin's definition of liberties for most of its analysis. At the least, the more balanced and pleasant position of Mandela has been made clear to the reader so as to avoid any implicit bias.

---

[63] Kant's analysis is also well-known in academic circles, but as we shall soon see, the structure of this Constitutional model seems to align much better with Berlin's liberties.

B. Sovereign-Liberties

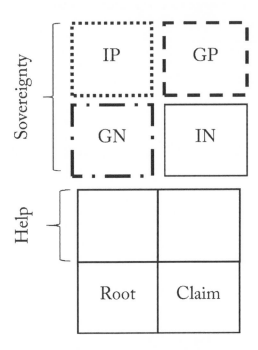

Fig-15—Berlin's liberties help define the Sovereign-liberties (IN, GP, GN & IP);
IN & GP liberty form Rule-of-Law and GN & IP liberty form Democratic-Inputs

It is possible to map Berlin's liberties onto the four sovereignty spaces in the model, and thus, identify a set of four *sovereign-liberties*. The four placements are depicted in Figure 15. As can be seen, IP liberty (Individual Positive liberty) is placed in the upper left, GP liberty (Group Positive liberty) is placed in the upper right, GN liberty (Group Negative liberty) is placed in the lower left, and IN liberty (Individual Negative liberty) is placed in the lower right.

Although Figure 15 is a simplified version of Figure 2 (only the Commerce-Right has been dropped), the line patterns enclosing the sovereignty spaces are from Figure 8a. Consequently, this matchup between Figure 15 and Figure 8a is an additional confirmation of the placements in Figure 15, for IP liberty corresponds to *Voluntary service*; GP liberty corresponds to *Promise to people*; GN liberty corresponds to *People's factions*; and IN liberty corresponds to *Individual privacy*. This matchup is summarized in the first and third columns of Table 5.2.

Table 5.2 Understanding the Sovereign-liberties		
Sovereign-liberties	Explanation of the Sovereign-liberties	Matching Space in Model (from Figure 8a)
Individual Negative Liberty (IN liberty)	Negative liberty with *Individual* as the agent	Individual privacy
Group Negative Liberty (GN liberty)	Negative liberty with *Group* as the agent	People's factions
Group Positive Liberty (GP liberty)	Positive liberty with *Group* as the agent	Promise to people
Individual Positive Liberty (IP liberty)	Positive liberty with *Individual* as the agent	Voluntary service

Further, a brief explanation for each of the four *sovereign-liberties* is given in the middle column of Table 5.2. IN and IP liberties assume *Individual* as the agent; GN and GP liberties assume *Group* as the agent. Although IN and IP liberties can be understood directly from Berlin's definitions (due to the agent being the individual), GN and GP liberties require additional explanation. While GP liberty is to be understood as part of the space containing mandatory state action (i.e., positive rights), GN liberty is to be seen as representing any group activity that cannot be interfered with by the state.

Let us now look at the sovereign-liberties based on whether they have negative and positive liberty strands. First, under negative liberty, we have GN and IN liberty. GN liberty can be understood as essential to all democratic political factions because, without it, there would be no negative liberty (i.e., existence) for democratic factions. IN liberty can be understood as the need to protect the negative liberty of individuals from both the state and the political factions. Legislature regulates the GN liberty space, and Judiciary regulates the IN liberty space.

Second, under positive liberty are GP and IP liberty. GP liberty arises from the past positions taken by GN liberty, provided those positions are free of conflict with IN liberty. By contrast, IP liberty arises more naturally; it is represented by those people who voluntarily choose to perform public service. If we view them together, public servants are free to use their IP liberty-based, discretionary judgment only to the extent that it does not infringe on the demand of the GP liberty. Executive-function regulates the IP liberty space, and the Control-function regulates the GP liberty space.

It was mentioned above that GP liberty implies the domain of positive rights.[64] Similarly, IN liberty implies the space represented by negative rights. Crucially, this means that while IN and GP liberties represent *rule-of-law*, GN and IP liberties may be thought of as *democratic-inputs*.

To be clear, the sovereign-liberties differ from Berlin's liberties in that the former is mostly concerned about the need for separation-of-powers in the government, whereas Berlin's definitions appear to be more an intuitive understanding of individual freedom.[65] This difference between

---

[64] GP liberty may be seen as a subset within positive rights since the latter was defined earlier as *mandatory state actions*.

[65] It must be noted that Berlin's definition invokes the concept of *group*, and therefore, it contains the seeds for a more complete analysis.

the two approaches becomes apparent if we attempt to categorize the four private spaces at the bottom of the model according to the four sovereign-liberties.

As is evident from the line patterns of Figure 15, the four private spaces are categorized as belonging to IN liberty, despite the fact that there is probably an equal amount of IP liberty present in those spaces. This sweeping categorization of private spaces as being IN liberty is unavoidable in the model—because as far as the model is concerned, it is only interested in the need to protect the private spaces from governmental interference.

C. Sovereignty-Grid (Dynamics of Sovereign-Liberties)

Let us now discuss some of the dynamics of the four sovereign-liberties by constructing a three-by-three grid. While the rule-of-law components (IN and GP) make up the rows, the democratic-input components (GN and IP) constitute the columns. The result is the nine-cell matrix shown in Figure 16, which we term the *sovereignty-grid*.

Before we explain the dynamics within Figure 16, we need to note that the two components within rule-of-law (IN and GP) have complementary properties. Similarly, democratic-inputs (GN and IP) are also thought to be complementary. The above complementarity assumptions can be supported by two separate arguments.

First, the assumptions can be explained via the Help-Right. The root element has a complementary relationship not only with its own claim space but also with the liberty space of the Help-Right present directly above it (refer to Figure 2). Similarly, the original Claim-Right space has a complementary relationship with the claim space of the Help-Right. These complementary relationships are projected onto the sovereignty space as well, which wind up creating the two complementary pairings within the four sovereign-liberties.

Second, the phenomenon of regulatory interdependence supports the complementarity assumption. IN regulator Judiciary and GP regulator Control-function cannot exist without the other also being present. For instance, the justice system functions adequately because the judges and police work as per the expectations of GP liberty. In addition, GP liberty can be misinterpreted to make the public servants seem like slaves to the *group*, save for the liberating presence of IN liberty, which guarantees the dignity of everyone. When it comes to the other pair of GN and IP, the GN regulator Legislature depends on the IP regulator Executive to handle administrative duties, just as the Executive depends on the Legislature to enact the necessary laws.

We may now examine Figure 16. The grid's corners show the interaction of each sovereign-liberty with the two sovereign-liberties that are not complementary to it. Consequently, the logic embedded in the grid forces its corners to either actively subvert rights or outright reject rights. Subversion of rights occur via lone "P" and "N" liberties in the top-right and bottom-left corners, and rejection of rights occur via lone "I" and "G" liberties in the bottom-right and top-left corners.[66]

---

[66] While it is probably easy to appreciate that the pure "P" and "N" liberties are equally problematic (they subvert the rights paradigm from opposite sides: action and inaction), it is perhaps more difficult to appreciate why the dangers associated with the pure "I" and "G" liberties are similar to each other (although they both reject the very concept of a rights paradigm). In particular, although the pure "G" liberty (rejects individuals) can be thought of as dystopian, and consequently, nobody espouses it, the pure "I" liberty (rejects the group and state) tends to be associated with utopian ideals, and consequently, at least some would argue that the "I" liberty is fundamentally good. In order to better appreciate the dangers of the pure "I" liberty, it may help to think of it as rejecting all norms, rather than just the state, which just happens to represent some important norms. Norms arise from people who agree on some common rules of interaction. It is this fundamental property that gets rejected by the "I" liberty, which is why it must be equated with the "G" liberty.

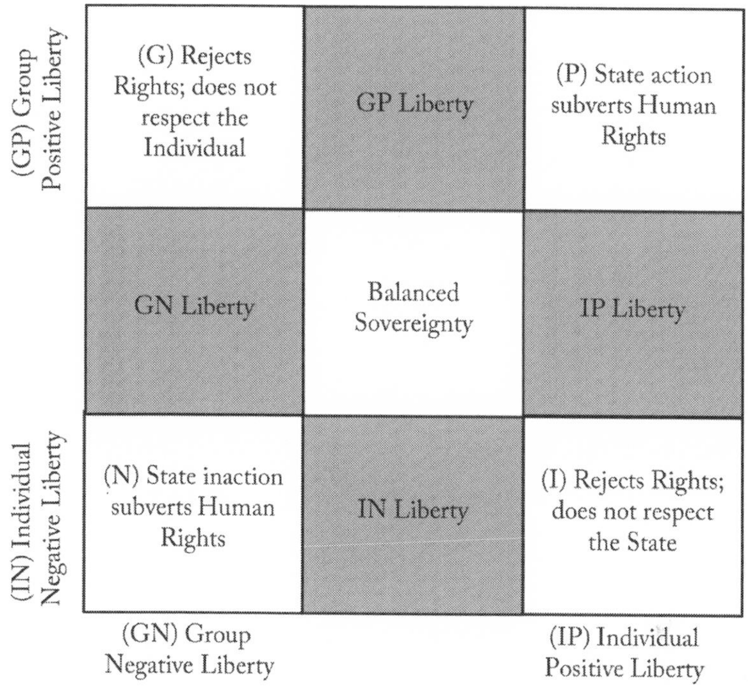

(G) Rejects Rights; does not respect the Individual	GP Liberty	(P) State action subverts Human Rights
GN Liberty	Balanced Sovereignty	IP Liberty
(N) State inaction subverts Human Rights	IN Liberty	(I) Rejects Rights; does not respect the State

(GP) Group Positive Liberty

(IN) Individual Negative Liberty

(GN) Group Negative Liberty

(IP) Individual Positive Liberty

Fig-16—Corners appear to reject Rights (G & I), or subvert Rights (P & N)

What this suggests is that when the democratic-input GN liberty wants to implement the rule-of-law (GP or IN liberties) by solely relying on its own initiative, it gets stuck in the problematic "G" or "N" liberty modes. Similarly, when the democratic-input IP liberty wants to implement the rule-of-law (GP or IN liberties) by solely relying on its own initiative, it gets stuck in the "P" or "I" liberty modes. Thus, the rule-of-law can only be achieved when both democratic-input components collaborate toward achieving it.

Let us take an even deeper dive to understand this situation. If we assume that the democratic-input of GN liberty prefers to implement the IN liberty rule-of-law, perhaps due to a preference for negative liberty, it follows that GN liberty prefers the "N" liberty mode to the "G" liberty mode. However, in order to get to IN liberty, it requires the collaboration of IP liberty. Similarly, if we assume that the democratic-input of IP liberty prefers to implement the GP liberty rule-of-law, perhaps due to a preference for positive liberty, it follows that IP liberty prefers the "P" liberty mode to the "I" liberty mode. However, in order to get to GP liberty, it will require the collaboration of GN liberty.

Further, just as collaboration of both democratic-inputs might be necessary to establish the rule-of-law regulators, presence of the two rule-of-law regulators might be necessary to ensure a stable working of the two democratic-inputs.

2. LOWER LIMITS
OF SOVEREIGNTY SPACE

The discussion in this second section is on the *lower limits* of sovereignty space. It will look at the minimum factors that are necessary for having stability in the system. We do this in two parts.

First, we inspect how to maintain the *minimum liberty space* for individuals. It refers to the minimum functionalities that are to be mandatorily delivered to all individuals by the government. Second, the *bottom-up stability* of the system is examined. This refers to the stability that is already naturally inherent in all human beings due to providence.

Further, as a heads-up to the coming discussion, while the *minimum liberty space* part will deal with aspects of rule-of-law, the *bottom-up stability* part will deal with prerequisites.

A. Minimum Liberty Space (Rule-of-Law Related)

Since the minimum liberty space represents the minimum functionalities that are to be guaranteed by government, we first look at the basic rationale for taxation, and then we examine what the minimum enforcement is that ought to be brought by governments against rights violations.

Incidentally, to defend our decision above to focus on taxes and justice, we can cite the views of Adam Smith. He is known to have identified the most important elements that a nation can focus on as taxes and justice: *"Little else is requisite to carry a state to the highest degree of opulence from the lowest barbarism but peace, easy taxes, and a tolerable administration of justice: all the rest being brought about by the natural course of things."*[67]

Rule-of-Law as the Rationale for Taxation

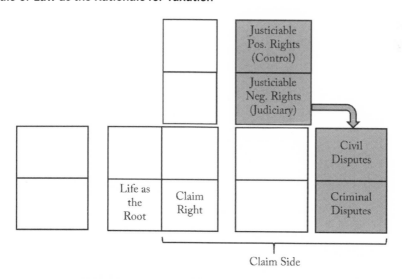

Fig-17a—Individuals may avoid Democratic-Inputs, but "Claim side" Rights should be provisioned universally

---

[67] This quote may not be from Smith's own published writings, but rather from a lecture he gave in 1755. It is quoted by Dugald Stewart in *Account of the Life and Writings of Adam Smith LL.D.*

Obviously, people are at complete liberty to choose their level of participation in society. Indeed, an individual may withdraw from public life to enjoy what might be a totally private life, but as far as the model is concerned, that individual would still be able to claim the full set of rights. This situation can be shown via Figure 17a since it highlights the fact that people have the option of not accessing the left half of the sovereignty space.

Since such laid-back people should still have full access to the rule-of-law regulators, the background settings for the enjoyment of liberty and rights need to be provisioned universally. As many of the necessary settings cannot be achieved without there being some public expenditure, it becomes necessary that taxes fund these activities. In other words, rationale for taxes is that the liberties enjoyed by the citizens will deteriorate if governments cannot maintain even the minimum level of liberty space that is expected by the citizens.

Thus, at a minimum, taxes are supposed to operationalize the shaded spaces in Figure 17a. Reducing the scope of public functions further will render the government ineffective in carrying out its core functions. It would not be an overstatement to say that the first call on taxes is from the cost structure of the criminal justice system. The cost structure of the defense forces is almost as important since the individual's need for security is both internal and external. However, the need for stability at the personal level is probably more important, since, without it, the nation would not exist in the first place.

Perhaps the civil justice system and the Control-function come next in the priority of government expenditure.[68] To sum up, taxation is primarily meant to ensure rule-of-law and external security.

---

[68] While government cannot force all civil disputes within its territory to be under the official government system, it must ensure there is capacity to deal with those civil complaints that do choose to come to it.

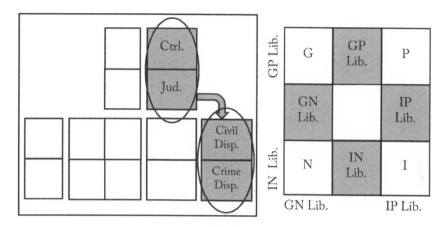

Fig-17b—Upper oval regulators resolve Rights violations in upper (G, P) corners; lower oval resolves lower (N, I) corners

Rule-of-Law as Enforcement against Human Rights Violations

Having dealt with taxes, we now turn to human rights violations. As mentioned earlier in Figure 16, each of the four corners of the sovereignty-grid are sources of rights violations. Since these violations must all be successfully resolved by the Constitutional structure, we should examine the situation via the layout shown in Figure 17b.

This new diagram has the Constitutional structure (Figure 17a) on its left and the sovereignty-grid (Figure 16) on its right. Some spaces of the Constitutional structure are highlighted by ovals, and it is these highlighted areas that ensure the rights violations in the corners of the sovereignty-grid can be effectively tackled.

To be specific about this, rights violations in the bottom corners of the sovereignty-grid are resolved by the structures for handling civil and criminal disputes. This ensures that there is a minimum level of state action—which is aimed at preventing the state from being just a mute spectator—if the residents raise alarm about some potential problems.

Similarly, rights violations in the top corners of the sovereignty-grid are resolved by the Control-function and the Judiciary's privacy protection function. They ensure that there is a certain level of state inaction, which is aimed at preventing the state machinery from overstepping the Constitutional bounds.

B. Bottom-Up Stability (Prerequisites Related)

To maintain the *bottom-up stability* of a system, the mandatory prerequisites for the system's very existence must be stable. In this particular case, interpretation would be that the stability already inherent in humans must not be tampered with.

When we examine the world via this outlook of *bottom-up stability*, apart from the obvious connection to medicine and biology, two specific areas come up, namely genomics and neural sciences. Accordingly, the bottom-up stability concerns in these two areas are briefly outlined below.

Human Genome Right

It can be argued that regulating genetic technologies,[69] especially in the domain of human germline engineering, is an area that the Constitutional structure should place at an even higher priority than the cost structure of the criminal justice system.[70]

---

[69] Apart from CRISPR-Cas9, there are also several other technologies in this area, like ZFN and TALENs.

[70] Germline engineering leads to heritable genetic changes, as opposed to changes that are patient-specific and not heritable.

This is because we need to look at what truly brings stability to decide the priority. Stability in the human biological space is a prerequisite for maintaining stability in the human social system. Consequently, human beings are far more important to the health of the system than even the minimum liberty space that ought to be provisioned by governments.

Apart from that systemic argument, there is a strong moral argument as well. All humans born into this world deserve to enjoy the same level of genetic stability that was naturally enjoyed by their ancestors. This is an inherently moral argument, which can be understood to be the negative right of human children to be protected from genetic experimentation. This can be termed as the *Human Genome Right*.

Human Conscience Right

There is another technology on the horizon that could prove, in time, to be just as dangerous as the already existing genetic technologies. This would be technology to interfere at the level of the brain's self-regulation capacity, which would mean interfering at the source of an individual's sovereignty over self.

Of course, any medical intervention done with the patient's consent should not be a cause for alarm, since such procedures may be necessary when they are essential to support or enable the body's normal functioning. However, the key factor to note here is that the approval and availability of medicines and associated procedures are regulated tightly. A lot of study is performed mandatorily so as to avoid potential harmful consequences to patients. Similarly, if more invasive brain-based technologies become available, or come close to existence in the commercial arena, they should be regulated at least as tightly as medicines. A strong case can be made that they should be regulated more tightly.

Indeed, it is entirely within reason to work toward a ban on this kind of technology if it can be taken beyond a certain medical threshold. This can be understood to be the negative right of the human brain's self-regulation to be protected from potentially invasive technologies. This can be termed as the *Human Conscience Right*.

6

———

People's Expectations
from Democracies

This chapter provides an analysis of people's expectations from democracies, which are understood to be systems that occupy the Stage-III level of the model. To start with, it is possible to analyze people's expectations from each evolutionary stage on three fronts:

1. Lower limits
2. Upper limits
3. Working dynamics

However, since the lower limits of democratic Stage-III are the same as the lower limits of sovereignty (covered in the previous chapter), that discussion can be skipped. This means that only the other two aspects of Stage-III democracies—working dynamics and upper limits—have to be covered here. We investigate these two areas in the two sections of this chapter.

1. WORKING DYNAMICS OF DEMOCRACIES

As part of understanding the working dynamics of Stage-III democracies, here we examine their stability from a couple of angles: stability vis-à-vis the outer environment, and stability vis-à-vis the inner forces. We may call the former *external-stability* and the latter *internal-stability*.

A. External-Stability:
Lincoln's Evolutionary Balancing

It may be recalled that Figure 1 and Figure 5 had suggested a situation where the root element is seemingly balanced against the final element. This can be depicted more directly, as shown in Figure 18, with the elements placed in between the first and the last element of the model forming the horizontal bar of the balance.

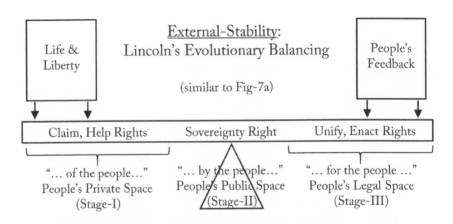

Fig-18—Lincoln's Evolutionary Balancing
(based on the first three evolutionary stages)

Perhaps almost poetically, the horizontal bar can be understood in terms of Lincoln's framing: *"of the people, by the people, for the people."* As private space cannot be interfered with by the government, or even by people in the public space, it is an unchangeable *"of the people."* As public space of sovereignty is the only area where ordinary people can directly exert their influence, it is *"by the people."* As legal space is where people's feedback can finally balance some unfair Stage-II structures, it is *"for the people."*

Attentive readers will notice that Commerce-Right, Regulation-Right, and Amendment-Right are not mentioned in the horizontal bar. While Amendment and Commerce-Right are not present in the diagram because they are not considered fully mature at Stage-III,[71] Regulation-Right is not mentioned in the diagram because it is thought to be implicitly present at each of the three stages.

From an academic and structural perspective, the three terms in Lincoln's quote can be explicitly mapped to the initial three evolutionary stages of Figure 7a. A more succinct version of that diagram is reproduced here as Figure 7b, for the reader's quick reference. In a manner that is reminiscent of Acemoglu and Robinson's theory in *Why Nations Fail*, Lincoln's quote also does not explicitly identify the need for Stage-IV. However, since Stage-IV is only a developmental extension from the model, the two approaches are relatively complete from the perspective of the model.

---

[71] Incidentally, Figure 18 makes a lot more sense when we place Commerce-Right in the third spot prior to Sovereignty-Right. Therefore, it is arguable that an alternate buildup to the model, where Commerce-Right is placed third, is superior to the buildup sequence we have used, at least in some respects. This will be examined in the second book of this series.

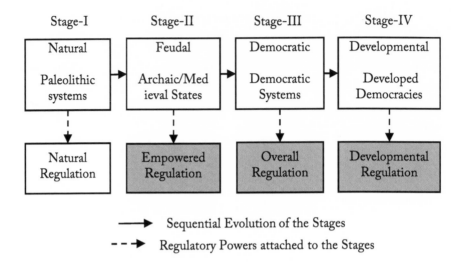

Fig-7b—*Evolution of Social Systems in four Stages*

The balance in Figure 18 is termed external-stability since it suggests a stabilization effect for the model with respect to the outer environment. For instance, the depicted balance is between the experienced life of the individual root elements and the collective decision-making capacity of all the root elements taken together.

However, rather than understanding the applicable forces as environmental-legal, it would be better to think of it as being merely *de facto-de jure* in nature. This is because the purely environmental component in the *de facto* forces is not large enough in most cases, unless one is already in the midst of an environmental disaster, in which case it may completely overwhelm the smaller human components.

This may explain why we have trouble responding effectively to long-term trends like climate change and environmental degradation. Unless people are already in the midst of an environmental disaster, they have a hard time perceiving the background environmental elements that are always present in the *de facto* forces.[72]

This leads to at least two challenges that have to be tackled effectively, if the model is to achieve an adequate level of stability, namely *environmental threats* and *democratic ineffectiveness*. These two challenges and their possible solutions are explained below.

a. *Environmental Threats (de facto* alone): The unavoidable existence of a larger environment raises the possibility of ecological disasters. Basically, it is not clear how the bottom-up feedback emanating from the experienced life of people can take steps sufficiently ahead of environmental disasters. After all, waiting to experience disasters at the appropriate scale will be life-threatening in many cases. These environmental threats could include things like water and food scarcity, declining irrigation capacity, declining soil fertility, loss of agricultural biodiversity, gradual impact from long-term climate change, energy shortages, geophysical events like earthquakes, weather events like hurricanes, outer space events like solar storms, etc.

Solution: The solution may be to have at least some Constitutional mechanism for systematically identifying and tackling such special situations, rather than to leave them completely up to the vagaries of people's ongoing democratic inputs. The solution must be capable of acting with

---

[72] Indeed, the background environmental setting is probably the most influential aspect behind regional differences in the private space values of people. After all, although human sentiments tend to be the same across all regions, the environmental setting differs significantly from region to region. Actually, this particular discussion might as well have been titled "Environmental Stability."

a long-term focus, in a way that is relatively insulated from short-term political pressures.

    b. *Democratic Ineffectiveness (de facto-de jure)*: This problem ignores the environmental component, and instead, examines how effectively information about the life experience of people can travel to the level of government in the form of people's feedback. In other words, as shown in Figure 18, it looks at the balance between the root element and the final element of people's feedback. Obviously, the effectiveness of this information flow is essential for democracy since, without it, the stability of the model vis-à-vis the *de facto* situation may collapse.

Solution: It seems almost tautological that any approach to tackle this problem would be about empowering democratic mechanisms to respond better to the bottom-up needs of the people. However, structure of the model is also important since it is necessary to encourage reason at the level of government. Perhaps people should be educated about the need for both *de facto* and *de jure* forces. Admittedly, this solution proposes nothing substantially new.

In particular, it should be noted that the balance shown in Figure 18 corresponds only to the problem of *democratic ineffectiveness*, and not to the problem posed by *environmental threats*. This is because, as noted earlier, environmental threats typically do not show up in people's lives, except when an outright disaster occurs. Therefore, the balance of Figure 18 should be understood only in terms of people's immediate life experience in democracies.

Nonetheless, it is interesting to note that an ability to solve one of

the two problems is likely to decrease the ability to solve the other problem. To be clear about this, if there is a high democratic effectiveness,
it may result in a lower ability to tackle environmental threats, since
people may not support high-fund allocations to address threats that
they have not yet directly experienced. At the other end, ensuring a high
level of preparedness against the environmental threats will likely come
at the cost of compromising fund allocations to other areas where people have more pressing daily needs. Therefore, it seems that the overall
solution must be to address the concerns of both without overindulging
either side.

It is also important to acknowledge that all democratic systems exist
so as to meet the people's bottom-up needs. As a consequence, the fund
allocation for meeting external threats can always be above some agreed-
upon limit,[73] but such a limit must surely be smaller in comparison with
the funding that can be moved based on the bottom-up demands coming
from the people.

B. Internal-stability:
Berlin-Mandela Sovereignty Balancing

This discussion on internal-stability will rely only on the four sovereign-
liberties that were discussed as part of Figure 15 and Figure 16. As explained
then, the sovereign-liberties do not rely on any external variable, but
instead appear to be internally controlled by either the agency of the
individual or of the *group*.

---

[73] Arguably, the priority of funding meant for addressing environmental threats should be about the
same as that of national defense expenditure, for the risks from the two are not all that different. This
point will also be argued for in Chapter Eleven.

The sovereign-liberty dynamics explained in the last chapter can also be illustrated via Figure 19, where a balance similar to Figure 18 is used to highlight the core tension present among the sovereign-liberties. The rule-of-law, represented by IN and GP liberties, forms the fulcrum of the balance, while the two weights are represented by GN and IP liberties.

Of course, as shown in Figure 19, the two weights can also be thought of as representing the two aspects of freedom present in Mandela's quote. Consequently, since both Berlin's liberties and Mandela's freedoms are present within Figure 19, internal-stability can also be called *Berlin-Mandela sovereignty balancing*.

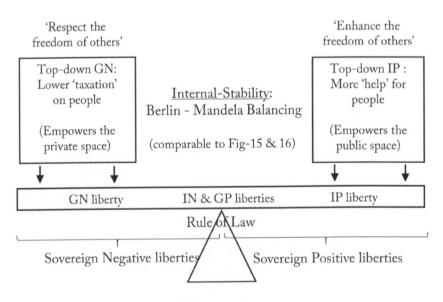

Fig-19—Sovereign-liberties bring an Internal-Stability to the Model

The main new information in Figure 19 is that top-down interpretation of GN liberty implies lower taxes as well as lower regulations, and it

empowers the private space activities. At the other end, top-down interpretation of IP liberty implies more help for people through the spending
activities of government, and it empowers the public space activities.

This leads to at least a couple of challenges that must be tackled effectively, if the model is to achieve an acceptable level of stability. These are
examined below.

a. *Biased Democracy*: This is basically the problem of balancing
   appropriately between the two weights represented by GN and IP
   liberties. Similar to the case of external-stability discussed earlier,
   where it was thought necessary to keep an even balance between
   de facto and *de jure* forces, here it is necessary to keep an even
   balance between the two democratic-inputs. Leaning too much in
   favor of either GN or IP liberty risks being regressive, since it might
   take the system back to the feudalism that was characteristic of
   Stage-II systems.[74]

Solution: When there is a relatively equal balance between the GN
and IP liberty, people emerge as the winner, instead of those who merely
seek to retain their power. For instance, such a balanced system is more

---

[74] While GN liberty populism risks a regression back to the Stage-II feudal system from which the system had progressed in the first place (implies at least a de-prioritization of people's democratic feedback,
which is not acceptable), IP liberty populism risks favoring something in fundamental opposition to the
earlier Stage-II feudal system, to the extent that the new system will even reject perfectly healthy Stage-III
or Stage-IV systems (for instance, this might involve rejecting the main goal of liberty and human rights
to favor some other dangerous ideology of democracy that cannot fit under this model). To be more clear
about this crucial point, while GN extremism can foster bottom-up violence (not governmental) so as to
entrench or fortify some social order (at its most violent, this can lead to ethnic and religious cleansing),
IP extremism can resort to top-down violence (governmental) so as to overthrow the existing social order
(at its most violent, this can lead to totalitarian governments). Paradoxically, despite the seeming difference in the two approaches, in both cases, the system will essentially collapse back to a Stage-II feudal
setup, which implies a system with authoritarian control.

capable of taking the people into the far better economic territory that is characteristic of Stage-IV systems. Accordingly, some constraints, like the Bicameral Legislature, should be inserted at the Constitutional level to avoid direct majoritarian control over democracies.

b. *Compromised rule-of-law*: It is likely that a balanced GN liberty will be inclined to give strong support to IN liberty since that tends to strengthen GN liberty. After all, IN liberty implies better protection for the private space. Similarly, a balanced IP liberty will be inclined to give strong support to GP liberty since that tends to strengthen IP liberty. After all, GP liberty implies better protection for the public space, especially through the CHQ factors and transparent processes around regulators. However, attempts by GN and IP liberty to exert exclusive influence over the IN and GP liberty spaces respectively, without collaborating with the other democratic-input component, could compromise the rule-of-law and lead to the situation shown earlier in Figure 16, wherein the lone "N" and "P" liberties begin to become active.

Solution: The straightforward approach would be to ensure that IP and GN liberties do not get sidetracked into representing the liberty-subverting "P" and "N" strands. Hopefully, this can be achieved by the simple expedient of treating the rule-of-law as independent from the people's democratic feedback, implying it should largely be insulated from the volatile sentiments of people. Moreover, both sides must respect the rule-of-law as a whole, rather than just the portion of it that might be better aligned with their position.

It is probably necessary to note here—to avoid any misunderstanding —that political party ideologies cannot be simplistically pigeonholed into the two buckets of GN and IP liberties. Instead, all well-functioning political parties will subscribe, on an almost equal basis, to both liberties. While GN liberty will motivate its members to work together, IP liberty will empower individuals to take up active political activities.

Thus, far from a political balance, Figure 19 is intended to convey the sense of balance that is necessary at the national and Constitutional levels. If we are forced to interpret Figure 19 as a political partisanship, it would require a system where only two parties are legitimate. Clearly, in a free democratic system, this would be out of the question.

2. UPPER LIMITS OF DEMOCRACIES

Upper limits might be a harder concept to grasp readily, when compared to the lower limits of systems. Fortunately, the areas falling under the umbrella of upper limits are rather similar in their structure to the areas already covered under the umbrella of lower limits. This makes it possible to discuss the concept of upper limits without too much trouble since we can anchor by referring to the earlier discussion on lower limits.

As may be recalled from the discussion in the last chapter, lower limits dealt with the two areas of *minimum liberty space* and *bottom-up stability*. In the case of upper limits, instead of looking at the *minimum liberty space* of individual—which is rule-of-law-related—we simply look at the *maximum liberty space*, which is democratic-input-related. Similarly, instead of looking at the *bottom-up stability*—which is about ensuring the stability of prerequisites enabling the system, we look at *top-down stability*, which is about ensuring peace in the external realm.

A. Maximum Liberty Space
(Democratic-Input Related)

When it came to minimum liberty space, the model relied on the rule-of-law regulators, namely Control-function and Judiciary, to achieve success. In contrast, when it comes to maximum liberty space, the model relies on the democratic-input regulators, namely Legislature and Executive, for getting desirable results. Indeed, during the lives of most people alive today, the activities implied by maximum liberty space might be better understood as the activities meant for merely increasing the liberty space.

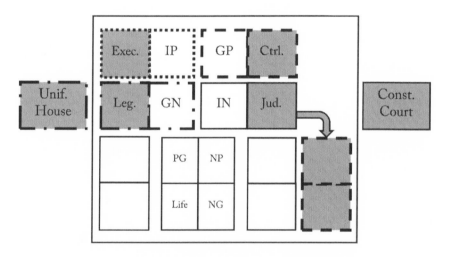

Fig-20a—Unification House & Constitutional Court are tied
to Sovereign-liberties GN & IN respectively

Although Figure 20a may seem similar to Figure 8a and 8b, it relies on the four sovereign-liberties, which were only introduced later on as part of Figure 15. Notably, this is the last time we will use the distinct-line patterns in the four sovereign spaces, mostly because they add an unnecessary layer of complexity to the diagrams.

On inspecting the line patterns used in Figure 20a, it is probably easy to appreciate that the second house of Legislature is staffed by those who adhere to some factions, and thus are represented by GN liberty. However, it may be harder to imagine the Executive-function being tied to IP liberty, since it suggests that Executive-function be more nonpolitical in nature, so as to gel with the nonpolitical attitude required from public servants.

Of course, Judiciary will find it much more comfortable to defend people's private space against such a nonpolitical Executive-function, compared to the situation they face currently, which frequently puts them in a position where they have to defend the private space against powerful political factions.

If Executive-functionaries are to be nonpolitical, they would have to be appointed by the head of government in a nonpartisan manner. Perhaps it can be arranged so that the nominations made by the head must be approved by the second house of Legislature,[75] which can be composed of representatives based on some metrics around proportional vote-share.

However, it is to be noted that proportional vote share can be used to fill the second house of Legislature only as long as the largest faction's vote-share is below some key threshold, like 50 percent. Otherwise, it will lead to majoritarian rule. Thus, while the first house can represent the

---

[75] If the approval is required only from the first house of Legislature, the Executive-function will be more political in its approach, and that runs a higher risk of violating the model. This is a risk more associated with parliamentary systems. To be clear, presidential systems also have drawbacks, one of which may be associated with the ODSI approach discussed in the next chapter.

faction with the plurality and be the Administrative House, the second house must represent non-majoritarian consensus and be the Unification House.[76]

Moreover, a full-time professional in that space is likely to increase the efficacy of the whole system. Since the head of government operates mostly outside of the spaces occupied by the four sovereign-liberties, it can be viewed as representing both IP and GN liberties at the same time. This flexibility may partly explain why it is granted the exclusive power to nominate the Executive functionaries.

B. Top-Down Stability
(Peace Related)

As mentioned earlier, here we look at *top-down stability* of the system, which is about ensuring peace in the realm of foreign affairs. As shown in Figure 20b, the spaces within foreign affairs can be described by the same four factors that were earlier used to describe the private space of individuals, namely Root, NG, PG, and NP. Although these terms were first introduced in Figure 8a, they are summarized for easy reference in Table 6 below.

---

[76] This is per the Unification-Right and *Federalist*, no. 51: *"divide the legislature into different branches; and to render them, by different modes of election and different principles of action, as little connected with each other as the nature of their common functions and their common dependence on the society will admit."*

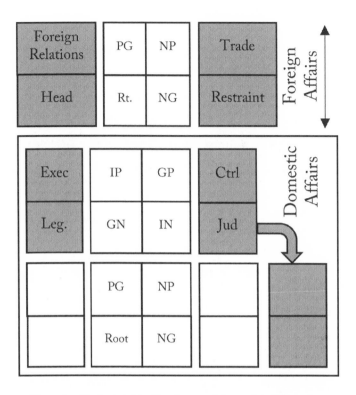

Fig-2ob—Restraint-function is meant for maintaining peace

Each of the four spaces in the foreign affairs space is regulated by the outer spaces placed adjacent to it. The space that regulates the Root space is the most important function at the foreign affairs level,[77] and it is occupied by the head of government. For the sake of convenience, we can also refer to this function as simply the *head*. The head might be a directly elected individual, or an indirectly elected one from the Administrative House. Of course, the power exercised by the head will be different in

---

[77] In domestic affairs, Legislature is far more powerful than the head, provided they have a majority position on the relevant issue. In fact, Legislature is so powerful that it alone has the power to reshape the Constitution.

the presidential and parliamentary systems, with the latter system giving the head a more direct access to the Legislature's taxation powers.

The Restraint-function regulates the NG space, and it is the second most important function at the level of foreign affairs. Restraint-function is mostly meant to check the tendency to initiate any untoward action in the foreign affairs space. In a slightly more general sense, Restraint-function is meant to maintain stability for the nation, with respect to the larger external environment. Obviously, this means Restraint-function is the Constitutional mechanism by which the threats in foreign affairs can be mitigated.[78]

In order to stand up to the head of government, the Restraint-function must be independent of it. It is perhaps not advisable to restrict its staffing to, say, the Justices from the Supreme Court, since the expertise garnered by the judges is specialized in a specific direction. Instead, the role of Restraint-function may be considered as open to any person, where the person is elected by an electorate that is more indirect than the electorate which elects the head.[79]

---

[78] Restraint-function also has to mitigate environmental threats, but this aspect is only brought out in the later chapters. It might be too early to discuss it here since additional material must be introduced first.

[79] At any rate, regardless of the electorate that is used, Restraint-function elections (and head of government elections) probably should not be plurality-based and must look to meet the 50 percent threshold. Most crucially, since the Restraint-function is elected in a more indirect manner than the head, it must be made relatively powerless in terms of domestic affairs. The opposite is also true; it is because the Restraint-function must mostly keep out of domestic affairs that it must be indirectly elected. It is necessary to avoid positions where there could be pernicious competition with the head.

Table 6 Functional Spaces within Foreign Affairs	
Foreign Affairs Regulators	Regulation of the Adjacent Functional Space
Head of Government	Regulates the root element space
Restraint-Function	Regulates the Negative Golden Rule (NG)
External Affairs	Regulates the Positive Golden Rule (PG)
Trade Function	Regulates the combined Golden Rule (NP)

The powers of the Restraint-function are debatable. For instance, it might be advisable to have the Restraint-function nominate the Control and Trade functionaries. After all, Restraint-function may represent, to some extent, the power bestowed by an electorate. That said, the nomination of Control and Trade functionaries probably does not carry any real power, for these positions are necessarily restricted to enforcing some aspects of the existing laws.

As shown in Figure 20b, in the case of Trade functionaries, this would mostly be about defending existing trade agreements. If some new agreements are to be envisaged, it must be under the initiative of the head. Of course, the confirmation of the nominees would be contingent on the opinion of the Unification House, or any other clearly delineated bipartisan process.

From a practical perspective, it is necessary to note here that the modern sea trade system among nations, which has prevailed since 1950 or so, is critical to preserve the global supply chains. The resources and technologies that are necessary in the modern economies do not lie within any single nation or small group of nations (nor is it ever likely to). There is also the fact that land transport is ten times less efficient than waterways.

Thus, if there is no system to replace the US Navy's security role, this could throw us back to a system of (mostly) ineffective domestic commerce. This is a very serious concern, and it suggests that this work, or any other work for that matter, cannot be considered practical or relevant if it fails to account for this problem.

Also, any system that does not already have twin power centers at the foreign affairs level, like the dual roles of prime minister and president, probably cannot implement the details of the Restraint-function, at least not without considerable effort. So it may be better to consider such Constitutional systems as outside the scope of the model.

3. LIMITS AND DYNAMICS

The discussions in the last two chapters can be summarized as shown in Table 7.1. Please note, details mentioned in the last chapter on sovereignty (upper row of table) holds for discussions in this chapter (bottom row) as well. Consequently, three points are worth emphasizing.

Table 7.1 People's Expectations from Sovereignty and Stage-III			
	Lower Limits	Working Dynamics	Upper Limits
Sovereignty	Minimum liberty space (Rule-of-law); Bottom-up stability (Prerequisites)	Sovereign-liberties Sovereignty-grid	
Stage-III (Democracy)	*Same as above*	*In addition to above:* External-stability and Internal-stability	Maximum liberty space (Democratic-inputs); Top-down stability (Peace)

First, the lower-limits discussion at the sovereignty level holds for the Stage-III level as well. Second, while the working dynamics at the sovereignty level hold for the Stage-III level as well, some additional dynamics (i.e., external- and internal-stability) are introduced in this chapter at the Stage-III level. Last, an upper-limits discussion is done only at the Stage-III level and not in the previous chapter on sovereignty.

7

People's Expectations from Developed Democracies

While the last two chapters dealt with people's expectations from sovereignty (Stage-II) and democracies (Stage-III) respectively, this chapter will deal with people's expectations from developed democracies (Stage-IV).

An overview of the discussions in the last two chapters are contained within the two upper rows of Table 7.2 (same contents as Table 7.1). Crucially, these learnings are perfectly valid and applicable for Stage-IV systems as well. However, there are some additional angles that become relevant at Stage-IV. It is these additional Stage-IV-specific details that are mentioned in the last row of Table 7.2.

Table 7.2 People's Expectations from the Evolutionary Stages			
	Lower Limits	**Working Dynamics**	**Upper Limits**
Sovereignty	Minimum liberty space (Rule-of-law); Bottom-up stability (Prerequisites)	Sovereign-liberties; Sovereignty-grid	
Stage-III (Democracy)	*Same as the above*	*In addition to the above:* External-stability and Internal-stability	Maximum liberty space (Democratic-inputs); Top-down stability (Peace)
Stage-IV (Developed Democracy)	*In addition to the above:* *Prerequisite* is about Org. board, and *rule-of-law* is Org. disputes resolution, etc.	*In addition to the above:* Berlin's liberties explain relations of some regulators and the ODSI approach	*In addition to the above:* Democratic-inputs act within the ODSI framework (e.g., contextual, conceptual)

In short, since this work primarily looks at three aspects of the evolutionary stages—namely lower limits, working dynamics, and upper limits—we shall look at these three aspects from the perspective of Stage-IV.

1. LOWER LIMITS OF DEVELOPED DEMOCRACIES

As shown in the *lower limits* column of Table 7.2, the Stage-IV analysis of lower limits uses the same analytical structure as earlier, namely maintaining the *prerequisites* and *rule-of-law*. As explained earlier, while prerequisites are necessary for ensuring *bottom-up stability*, rule-of-law is necessary for ensuring *minimum liberty space*. We examine these two areas below.

A. Bottom-Up Stability (Prerequisites Related)

In order to discuss bottom-up stability at the Stage-IV level, we shall use Figure 21.

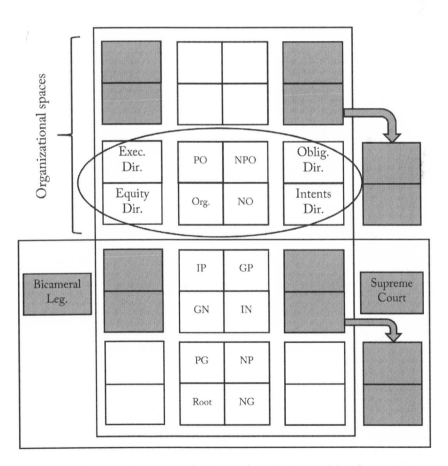

Fig-21—Organizational spaces (inside oval) are the Prerequisites for Stage-IV

Notably, since this discussion is meant to deal exclusively with the *prerequisites* that are necessary for accessing Stage-IV, the relevant spaces in Figure 21 are highlighted by an oval.

The spaces lying within the oval are considered part of the *prerequisites* for accessing the Stage-IV level of the model. The regulators connected to these spaces are called *embedded-regulators*; these regulators must be embedded on the boards of their respective organizations.[80] Incidentally, all eight spaces inside the oval come under the rule-of-law, dealing with privacy.

Job Profiles of the Four Directors

There appears to be four types of Directors on the boards of organizations, namely Equity Director, Intent Director, Executive Director, and Obligations Director. Just as the individual's private spaces (Root, NG, PG, NP) were defined with the help of the Golden Rules,[81] we can do the same for the four Directors as well. The Equity Director regulates the space of commercial organization itself; the Intent Director regulates the negative Golden Rule at the organizational level (NO); the Executive Director regulates the positive Golden Rule at the organizational level (PO); and the Obligations Director regulates the combined Golden Rule space at the organizational level (NPO).

---

[80] In the absence of laws distinguishing between formal and informal organizations, the default distinction may be that informal organizations derive their justification from private property laws and the local social norms on the daily wages of workers. However, when the commerce of the organization becomes large enough, it becomes necessary to have specific laws concerning the governance of the organization, so as to prevent systemic problems. Even so, some distinctions will still have to be made between various categories like micro, small, and medium enterprises (MSME) and the larger organizations.

[81] Please refer to Figure 8a or Table 6 for the details.

The Equity Director represents the long-term interests of shareholders, which can perhaps be thought of as the organization's fidelity to its mission of being able to continue its promised level of service for its customers. Although the shareholding percentages determine who will be the Equity Director,[82] the metrics that are to be used to gauge their performance are not as clear.[83]

The Intent Director has a complex task involving a diverse set of elements: financial audits, lobbying practices, tax compliance, legal compliance, protection of micro shareholders,[84] and even avoidance of bad faith in services to stakeholders. Although it is far from obvious how these disparate elements are to be prioritized, audit and legal matters are probably the areas that must be attended to first.

The Executive Director is the one charged with helping the customer and is responsible for customer satisfaction. They handle the execution of all customer-related activities of the organization, which probably implies all organizational activities that are not allocated to the other Directors.

The Obligations Director looks after all noncritical contractual obligations of the organization, especially those with its employees and partners.

---

[82] Representation should be as per some norms related to the shareholder percentage. The situation seems similar to the Unification House that may get filled based on proportional vote-share. Just as there must be measures for protecting minority factions in the case of the Unification House, there must be some measures for protecting minority shareholders as well. If a majority faction with more than 50 percent shareholding exists, which raises the possibility of undue pressure on Independent Directors, perhaps there can be a seat reserved for the largest minority faction as well. Obviously, this would need some conditions like the threshold levels to be set. However, in most cases, equity holders can easily exit their positions, and consequently, the minority shareholders within companies are nowhere near as vulnerable as people belonging to minority factions.

[83] For instance, although return on equity is more important than most other metrics, it cannot capture some important details regarding the organization's performance.

[84] Micro shareholders are assumed to be those shareholders who are not directly represented by the Equity Directors, even if there is a Director dedicated to representing a large minority position (refer to footnote 82).

Complaints that are mission-critical, especially those sourcing from customers, shareholders, and the law, can be handled by the Directors responsible for those areas. However, situations that become grave enough to threaten the viability of the organization probably should be treated as the combined responsibility of all the Directors. That said, even if activities of an employee union are judged to be mission-critical, they may primarily be handled by the Obligations Director.[85] The entry, conduct, and exit of all employees and partners should be their responsibility.

Independent and Non-Independent Directors

Although all four Directors must be committed to the Constitutional rule-of-law and the Golden Rules in the commercial context,[86] there is a difference between Independent and Non-Independent Directors. While the Independent Directors are expected to focus more on the rule-of-law, the Non-Independent Directors are expected to focus more on applying the Golden Rules in the commercial context.

The Independent Directors will prioritize compliance with the passive background settings first, even over the active foreground requirements of the organization itself. This would stem from the fact that they are duty bound to ensure compliance with the rule-of-law, regardless of the organization's own interests. The Non-Independent Directors work within these constraints put on the organization and still find innovative ways to serve the customers.

In case the founder or promoter of the organization is still active, there

---

[85] Unions are probably necessary to protect employees from exploitation, and as such, they probably should continue to exist even after the Obligations Directors are appointed.

[86] As discussed in Chapter One, Golden Rules in the commercial context may be viewed as primarily aimed at helping customers, provided the laws of the state and the rights of citizens are not violated.

is the option of clubbing the roles of Equity and Executive Directors. Similarly, there may also be a need for clubbing the roles of Intent and Obligations Directors in some situations, perhaps with smaller organizations that have only recently become active.

Of course, if we club the responsibilities belonging to the Intent and Obligations Directors together, that leads to the current role of the Independent Director, which is the default setting in organizational boards today. The model suggests that such an understanding of the Independent Director is meant for resource-poor smaller organizations, rather than larger organizations.

Nomination and Expenses of Independent Directors

At a superficial level of analysis, it may seem as though the tax rationale argument presented in Chapter Five (taxes are necessary to ensure rule-of-law) can be extended to require that all the expenses related to Independent Directors be provided for from the taxes collected. After all, Independent Directors represent the rule-of-law and might even be part of immunity-regulators.

However, it is even clearer that governments cannot be allowed to interfere in the boards of organizations, since that would violate the understanding gained regarding the responsibility of the Judiciary to provide fundamental protection to the negative rights of individuals and organizations.[87] Governments can only put in place laws and policies to ensure a level playing field for competition between organizations.

---

[87] Incidentally, government cannot directly appoint Independent Directors, since that would violate the *independence* of immunity-regulators. However, it is unnecessary to stress the immunity angle here, since an even larger point is being made, which is about government's inability to interfere at the level of all Directors.

This seems to suggest the position that while people are not expected to bear the expenses of Independent Directors, people can set the general qualification criteria for them via an appropriate legal process. In other words, the task of selecting appropriate Independent Directors and bearing their associated expenses can be done only by the existing board.

B. Minimum Liberty Space
(Rule-of-Law Related)

In Chapter Five, we identified rule-of-law as the key enabler for maintaining *minimum liberty space* because it is essential for resolving human rights violations (refer to Figure 17b). Similarly, rule-of-law at the Stage-IV level is also the enabler of minimum liberty space at its level because it is essential for creating the economic liberty expected at the Stage-IV level.

Thus, at a minimum, taxes are supposed to operationalize all the spaces within the Constitutional structure shown in Figure 22. Like Figure 17a, this figure also does not contain the spaces corresponding to democratic-inputs. This omission serves to emphasize the freedom of the ordinary people, in that they may choose not to participate in those optional spaces. Of course, to enact on taxes and to collect it in an effective manner, it will be necessary to have the Legislature and the Executive as well.

Reducing the functions beyond what is shown in the diagram will render Stage-IV ineffective in facilitating economic development. It would not be an overstatement to say that the first call on taxes at the commercial level is from the cost structure of the commercial justice system.

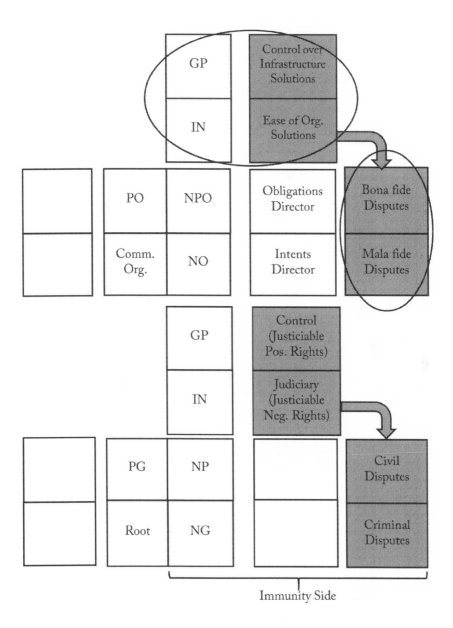

*Fig-22—Rule-of-law spaces related to Organizations
are shown inside the two ovals*

Earlier, it was stated in the context of Stage-III that the cost structure of the Judiciary function is more important than that of defense forces since the individual citizen has no need for external security if the internal security itself fails. Similarly, high productivity in the commercial arena, which is ensured by the Judiciary protecting the organizational private space, is more important than the defense function at the Stage-IV level. Without a certain minimum level of organizational efficiency, the nation would not be able to continue functioning at the high economic level expected at the Stage-IV level.

The cost structure of Control-function probably comes next in priority, right after the cost structure of the defense forces. Incidentally, it is arguable that rule-of-transparency at the level of developmental extension must include enabling the rise of MSMEs (Micro, Small and Medium Enterprises) by giving them transparency in terms of the necessary compliances. It is not advisable for public servants to have the power of imposing new compliances unless they can assure that the transparency level (from the perspective of organizations) is maintained. Regulatory burden on smaller organizations should be lower than that on larger organizations. Although this might not fit under the standard CHQ schema, it fits quite well under the rule-of-transparency.

However, the public spaces in the commercial arena continue to be characterized by the people's sovereign-liberties of IN and GP liberties (upper oval in Figure 22). This is because those public commercial spaces are controlled by the people through their rule-of-law regulators, and not by mechanisms belonging to the commercial organizations.

Commercial Justice System at Stage-IV

When we look at *Ease of Org. Solutions* in Figure 22, we come to the commercial justice system at the Stage-IV level. Obviously, IN liberty within
the oval in Figure 22 also holds for private organizational spaces. This
implies that the Judiciary has to protect the organizational private space
from encroachments by the other three empowered-regulators, who may
even say that they are acting on behalf of the people. However, since
organizations are artificial constructs that cannot be granted *individual
rights*, it is difficult to say how the Judiciary should approach the defense
of organizational private space.

Perhaps, since private organizational space is based on the *autonomy*
enjoyed by people in private commercial spaces, that fact can serve as the
rationale for Judiciary's structural responsibility to protect the organizational private spaces from the other three regulators.[88] Indeed, if board
autonomy is not present in law and protected by courts, it means that the
country is resolutely stuck at Stage-II or Stage-III, instead of progressing
gradually toward Stage-IV.[89]

Also, Judiciary will have to resolve disputes not just between organizations, but also between individuals and organizations. These
disputes could be between the organization and its customers, employees, shareholders, and others. If complaints from shareholders or citizens get escalated to the Judiciary, it might be a failure of the Intent

---

[88] However, the board can be reconstituted in some special situations, like serious fraud or systemic risks
to the country. This would, of course, require the consent of the Judiciary.

[89] Incidentally, while organizational spaces are modeled from the human behavior in the commercial
spaces, it is conceivable that some of their characteristics are also derived from Stage-III regulators.
Indeed, maybe it is the non-majoritarian structure of the Bicameral Legislature which ensures the protective norms for minority shareholders.

Directors. Similarly, if complaints from customers or employees get escalated, it might be a failure of the Obligations Directors.[90] However, it is assumed that any *mala fide* treatment given to customers and employees falls in the former category since most citizens will find such treatment objectionable.

Just as Intent Directors have a responsibility toward micro shareholders, Obligations Directors certainly have some responsibility toward an organization's customers. It is because of this additional responsibility of the Obligations Directors, that it is not advisable to think of them exclusively as the voice of the employees. Rather, they represent the rule-of-law, and therefore are constrained to act in a manner that keeps them within the ambit of relevant laws and the Constitution.

Control-Function's Infrastructure Responsibilities

When we look at *Control over Infrastructure Solutions* in Figure 22, we come to Control-function's infrastructure responsibilities. The details are set out in Table 4.3. Of course, these responsibilities are already present and active at the Stage-II and Stage-III levels. But they become more visible and important at the Stage-IV level.

---

[90] However, while there may be complaints about outstanding arrears from employees in the event of bankruptcies, if an organization goes into bankruptcy, it is the fault of the entire board. In a bankruptcy process, it is the secured lenders (typically banks) who have priority over other stakeholders, like partners, employees, shareholders, etc. This may be because the secured lender's priority is sourcing directly from the mandatory laws of the country, which is more important than settling the remaining outstanding issues sourcing from the voluntary activities done by the organization. At the same time, since banks represent the laws of the land, it is possible that banks may not be allowed to place their nominees on the boards of organizations they lend to, for that may be tantamount to governmental interference in organizational boards. This last point is less sure and needs more examination.

Table 4.3 Stage-II/III/IV Control-Function's Regulation of Infra-Organizations		
Factors	Functional Area	Relevant Parameters
Cost	Infra. Cost/Audit	Contractual payments to infra-organizations
Quality	Recruitment, Retention	Merit in experience, No passive bias
Honesty	Infra. Org. Ombudsman	No active conflict of interest (e.g., cost inflating)

Although the Control-function's job in the infrastructure space is mostly about monitoring the same set of generic performance parameters listed in Table 4.1, the difference is that public servants are replaced by commercial organizations in voluntary infrastructure roles (i.e., infra-organizations).

The first two factors in Table 4.3, namely Cost and Quality, are probably self-explanatory. However, it is worth noting that the "no passive bias" associated with the Quality factor might perhaps be better understood as a proximity to problematic lobbies. As for the third factor of Honesty, what we mean is that infra-organizations should not engage in active conflict-of-interest areas, like inflating their project costs or indulging in monetary lobbying.

Besides the three control parameters mentioned above, infra-organizations are also subject to the regulations imposed by the Legislature and the dispute resolutions done by the Judiciary. Thus, infra-organizations are like public servants, in that both parties have to adhere to regulations from all four of the empowered-regulators. By contrast, normal commercial organizations and citizens are mostly concerned only with the Legislature and Judiciary (an exception being their capacity to raise grievances with the Ombudsman).

Areas of public infrastructure could include food, water, education, healthcare, public utilities, and more. It is also important to keep in mind that disruptive improvements may be possible in these spaces. An example is the rise of broadband services. Therefore, the model must be flexible to account for such productive changes taking place in the economy. In this regard, it will be the responsibility of the Executive and Legislature to bring such disruptive improvements into the public infrastructure domain, for the Control-function has a more restricted mandate.

At first glance, it may seem as though the Control-function is only restricted to carrying out the wishes of the Legislature as expressed in lawful enactments, but the restriction on the function may go further than that. As mentioned earlier in Chapter Three, since the responsibilities of Control-function must be made justiciable to the citizens, it is possible that the Control-function cannot seek to go beyond enforcing the CHQ factors and ensuring the rule-of-transparency.

2. WORKING DYNAMICS
OF DEVELOPED DEMOCRACIES

As noted in Table 7.2 at the start of this chapter, some working dynamics of sovereignty are understood via sovereign-liberties (Figure 15) and the sovereignty-grid (Figure 16). Further, working dynamics of Stage-III can be understood via external-stability (Figure 18) and internal-stability (Figure 19). It is crucial to note that all four of these dynamics continue to *dominate* at the level of Stage-IV as well.

As a result, if new information is to be presented regarding working dynamics of Stage-IV, it must be done from some other angles. Here, two such approaches are discussed. First, the dynamics of Stage-IV regulators can be examined in terms of Berlin's original liberties (not the four sovereign-liberties). Second, the possibility of a synergy between the two Stage-IV democratic-inputs are explored.

A. Berlin's Liberties in the Stage-IV Regulatory Spaces

In Figure 6, the natural regulators present in individuals and their parallel Stage-IV regulators present in organizations are termed as embedded-regulators, partly to distinguish them from the empowered-regulators present immediately above them. Using Berlin's basic definition of negative and positive liberty, it is possible to define at least three relationships among the embedded- and empowered-regulators.

First, while the embedded-regulators enjoy full, negative liberty from the empowered-regulators, they exercise positive liberty with regard to the private functional spaces they regulate. Second, while the empowered-regulators enjoy negative liberty with respect to the Bicameral Legislature and the Supreme Court, they exercise positive liberty with regard to the public spaces they regulate. Third, the empowered-regulators next to the sovereignty spaces exercise positive liberty over the empowered-regulators next to the commercial spaces.

All three of these inter-relationships among the regulators are able to exist because they are adequately protected by the appropriate levels of Judiciary. For instance, the first relationship may not need any interventions at the level of the Constitutional side of the Supreme Court.

Admittedly, this is an easy description of the model's best-case scenario at the level of Stage-IV. By contrast, the description of average case

scenarios, especially with regard to Stage-III and its relatively poor organizational spaces, will be harder.[91]

B. Democratic-Inputs for Economic Prosperity: ODSI Approach

Stage-IV is considered capable of delivering economic prosperity of a kind
that would not be possible even at the Stage-III level. Therefore, there is
a need to be clear about the mechanism by which we can achieve such
economic results.

The economic functioning behind the Stage-IV level can be understood in terms of the ODSI approach, where the four letters stand for
Ownership, Discretion, Services, and Infrastructure. Incidentally, these
four factors are present at the Stage-II and Stage-III levels as well, but
a different level of synergy needs to be unleashed at the Stage-IV level
since the expectations are higher.

---

[91] The average case scenarios within Stage-II systems probably should not be delved into in too much
detail by the model, for that runs the risk of legitimizing those arrangements.

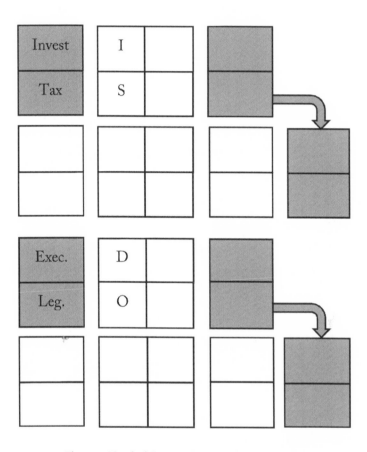

Fig-23—Head of Government may be responsible
for the ODSI approach

The above-mentioned four factors have been placed in their concerned cells in Figure 23. As can be seen, the ODSI factors do not cover rule-of-law spaces. Instead, they cover only the democratic-input spaces of GN and IP liberties. Consequently, ODSI has to be understood in terms of the regulatory activities around the two democratic-inputs. This means that since the head of government is the only position having the required visibility across the two democratic-inputs,[92] it is best placed as the function responsible for the overall working of the ODSI framework.

The four factors of ODSI can be explained as follows. People in the public space adjacent to the Legislature can be thought of as the *owners*. Executive-function is responsible for extracting energy from the environment and delivering it to the people, in a form that is most conducive to their overall welfare. For instance, in an ideal situation represented by advanced Stage-IV systems, this might even include Universal Basic Income (UBI).

To perform its function, the Executive is given the responsibility to make *discretionary* decisions, which can be based on the inputs from existing public servants or other experts who are tasked with providing the necessary information.[93] While Legislature decides how much taxes to collect from the profitable agents who deliver the commercial *services* demanded by the citizens, the Executive-function decides which investments are likely to be productive enough in the *infrastructure* sector. Thus, the focus is on the SI part of the ODSI approach.

Since investments would have to be made in such a manner that the productive capacity of the economy does not diminish over time, a key task would be to ensure sufficiently high EROI is maintained over time. For those wondering what EROI is, it is very much like the well-known ROI (Return on Investment) metric used in business. We can immediately grasp

---

[92] Admittedly, in the presidential system, the head has direct control over only two of the four factors (Discretionary and Investments). It is only in the parliamentary system that the head has reasonable control over all four areas. Therefore, as far as the presidential system is concerned, it may not be an overstatement to say that the responsibilities of the head are mostly centered on the two domains of external affairs and infrastructural investments.

[93] The inputs can also come from the infra-organizations. Indeed, certain types of inputs can only be provided if the agent has a detailed understanding of confidential situations.

the meaning of EROI from its full form—*Energy Return on Energy Invested.*[94]

Obviously, apart from investing into areas promising high EROI outcomes, a lot of work would also have to be done in the surrounding infrastructure space. For instance, the term *infrastructure* denotes hard, physical aspects, like road, rail, ports, airports, waterways, telecom, power, and other utilities. That said, its use in this model definitely includes the soft biological aspects as well, including food, water, shelter, education, healthcare, biodiversity, and pollution.[95]

However, it is entirely up to the Legislature of a particular country to decide what will come under the heading of infrastructure, because the decision implies having to deploy some of the collected taxes into that area of activity.

3. UPPER LIMITS OF DEVELOPED DEMOCRACIES

As noted in Table 7.2 at the start of this chapter, *upper limits* can be examined in two parts: the maintenance of *maximum liberty space* and the maintenance of *top-down stability.* At the level of Stage-IV, the former hinges on understanding the ODSI approach, which has just been explained, but the latter requires us to understand the connection between Constitution and the sciences, which unfortunately falls outside the scope of this book.

Therefore, as far as this book and chapter are concerned, we must limit ourselves to discussing only the area of *maximum liberty space.*

---

[94] Those wanting a detailed understanding of the EROI concept should refer to the works of Charles Hall.

[95] We should distinguish between programs requiring large, upfront expenses and those requiring large, recurring expenses. While the former can be counted as infrastructure (provided the later maintenance expenses are minor), the latter ought to be counted as public welfare. Obviously, the best investment to make is in high-EROI energy technology, since the returns will dwarf even the large, upfront expenses.

A. Maximum Liberty Space (Democratic-Inputs Related)

Stage-III dealt with *maximum liberty space* by ensuring the proper regulation of democratic-inputs, namely the Legislature and Executive-functions. Stage-IV also deals with the task via the democratic-inputs. However, in this case, those inputs act within the ODSI framework.

The ODSI approach can be interpreted in two ways—contextual and conceptual. While the former is a practical take on the quickly approaching crises related to the use of fossil fuels, the latter is a more theoretical take on the planet's finite limits.

Contextual Perspective
(Practical Take on the Looming Fossil Fuel and Climate Crises)

From a contextual and historical perspective, since the advent of the industrial revolution, fossil fuels have triggered a huge boom in both the population and freedom of humans. In parallel with the boom in our population, we have successfully moved in a large number of countries from the Stage-II level, represented by historical feudal societies, to Stage-III systems represented by Constitutional democracies.

If the supply of these fossil fuels can no longer be increased, perhaps due to ecological limits like climate change or liquid fuel scarcity, it is doubtful whether the current Stage-III systems will sustain. Things are fragile enough that just the lack of an ability to increase the energy supply on a consistent basis could trigger a collapse back to Stage-II, along with truly unprecedented human suffering. The only alternative is that we somehow rise to and then stabilize at the level of Stage-IV, because that is where the energy supply required for stability might be achievable via the ODSI approach. In contrast, Stage-III offers no special ability on the energy front.

This higher capacity at the Stage-IV level is mostly due to the productive enterprise unleashed by its commercial organizations. In particular, it is the dynamics of infrastructure present in the ODSI framework, which can increase the energy per capita availability within the nation, by enlisting the services of infra-organizations in the energy sector.

If we fail to enable a different energy paradigm than the current system enabled by fossil fuels, the maximum liberty space enabled by our Stage-IV systems would not reach its full potential. It would have to be viewed as limited by historical and contextual circumstances.

Conceptual Perspective
(Theoretical Take on Our Finite Planet and Its Fragile Ecology)

Even if the looming fossil fuel and climate crises are resolved, if we assume the steady increase in energy demand continues unabated thereafter, it will cause another crisis in the near future, even if only due to the somewhat distant finite limits of the planet.[96] However, there is also the more pressing possibility for an ecological crisis, where the biosphere's civilization-supporting systems would degrade to such an extent that a large energy supply, on its own, would no longer be adequate.

This ecological degradation might be related to any number of crucial things: species loss, forest loss, fertile soil loss, and loss of high-grade ores. Therefore, the increase of the energy supply achieved at Stage-IV cannot be unmindful of the planet's ecological limits. There will be a point beyond

---

[96] It might be worthwhile to listen to Professor Bartlett's lectures on exponential limits to understand the dynamic that is at work here: https://youtube.com/watch?v=F-QA2rkpBSY (Last accessed on May 3, 2022).

which further increases of the energy supply will endanger the ecological limits. The point of that energy per capita availability is the maximum liberty space that can be attained.

Indeed, maintaining the maximum liberty space is all about recognizing this point of the highest energy availability that is maintainable, and then maintaining it by not allowing declines in the energy supply or pursuing additional destabilizing increases. This is easy to say but hard to achieve in practice.

Perhaps a certain portion of the taxes can be devoted to maintaining ecology or restoring ecology to its natural state. In other words, the planet's ecology should reach a situation where it maintains itself with no artificial energy inputs from us. Ideally, this allocation for restoring ecology should be accorded the same priority level as the defense expenses. In this scenario, it is only the tax left over from that initial allocation to ecology that will be available to the government for other public projects.

Finally, in summary of this discussion on the contextual and conceptual perspectives, one of the few, sure things is that an approach like the ODSI is desirable, and that it is best achieved by paying attention to maintaining high EROI metrics, which will require carefully targeted R&D in the energy sector.

8

Avoidable
Misinterpretations

This chapter will discuss the misinterpretations that might arise in connection with the content presented in the second part of this book. Since three chapters (five, six, and seven) have been covered in the second part of this book, we discuss the issues relating to those chapters in three separate sections.

1. MISINTERPRETATIONS RELATED TO CHAPTER FIVE

Some of the more important misinterpretations to avoid in Chapter Five can be listed as follows:

1. Force-fitting the model as being indifferent to religions
2. Force-fitting the model as being biased in favor of negative liberty

3. Force-fitting new root elements in the spaces belonging to GN liberty and commercial-objective

4. Force-fitting the fundamental protection of private spaces as implying something more than the Human Conscience Right

Attempting to Force-Fit the Model as Being Indifferent to Religions

Far from being indifferent about religions, the model welcomes such traditions in the private space of people but discourages them in the public space. To be specific with regard to the private space, the model holds that spiritual beliefs like religions tend to promote pro-social behavior that is in line with the Golden Rules, which is something that is difficult to achieve in other ways. After all, governments cannot interfere in the private space of people.

With regard to the public space, the model is clear that religions should not intrude into the level of Berlin's positive liberty.[97] There is a good reason for this. Although religions are desirable when they promote compassion and kindness at the private level, not keeping them out of the governance area could lead to some extreme positions being taken up, which would potentially be bad for the cause of peace.[98]

---

[97] This is easier said than done, though. People's democratic feedback has components that correlate with people's religious affiliations. Constitutional structure must nevertheless attempt to reduce the influence from this quarter. Some approaches have been mentioned as part of the discussion on factions in Chapter Three.

[98] However, religious states cannot be directly discussed here because the situation cannot be modeled theoretically. A religious state is a problem that has been practically observed—not theoretically modeled. Moreover, even if religious states operate with some democratic structures, their extreme policy positions might remain. The examples of Israel and Iran are worth considering.

Moreover, religious states could potentially reject key aspects of the UDHR-like norms, and perhaps even the liberty-enhancing approach that has been suggested for the building of Constitutional models. In other words, when it comes to religious states, this Constitutional model cannot be applied.

Attempting to Force-Fit the Model as Biased in Favor of Negative Liberty

Although Berlin says both negative and positive liberties are equally valid, it is clear that he was not as wary of the potential for negative liberty's misuse as he was of the potential for positive liberty's misuse. In Berlin's defense, he was probably thinking of negative liberty in terms of IN liberty, as opposed to the GN liberty that this work identifies.

IN liberty probably cannot be misused to reduce other people's freedoms in a systematic manner, but an inchoate GN liberty can subvert the rule-of-law represented by IN liberty. And in doing so, it would regress into the lone "N" liberty, which is probably the main form in which excessive negative liberty manifests itself.

Not just that, but without the self-correcting balance of nonviolent democracies, positive liberty introduced by democracies could intrude into people's private spaces, and thus, damage the negative liberty of the people. Berlin is perhaps anticipating this danger with his wariness of positive liberty. However, he may have been thinking of the application of positive liberty at the feudal level. Stage-III democracy actually corrects the excesses in the Stage-II system by implementing the dual control between Bicameral Legislature and Supreme Court.

Further, in Acemoglu and Robinson's work *Why Nations Fail,* they give a good descriptive account of two categories—absolutist regimes from medieval Europe and outright state failures like Somalia, Haiti, Afghanistan, etc. These two categories seem to align with extreme positive liberty and extreme negative liberty, respectively. If this hypothesis about the alignment of excessive positive and negative liberty with the historical examples is broadly correct, both forms of excess should be considered equally dangerous to human well-being.[99]

In addition, the cul-de-sac blocking progress to Stage-III, which is represented by majoritarian democracies where a political party consistently gets greater than 50 percent of vote-share, may be aligned with excessive negative liberty.[100] However, this need not be the case always. It is possible that even in those social contexts where majoritarian vote-share is the norm, or has occurred frequently in the past, rule-of-law may still hold up tolerably well.

To sum up, since this work is limited to how the systems behave from the Stage-III level onward, it has to treat both types of excesses as equally dangerous to the Constitutional model and human liberty. Accordingly, the position of this work is that we need to be equally wary of the potential for excess from both liberties.

---

[99] In the case of excessive negative liberty, it might manifest itself as vigilante justice, with people attempting to take the administration of law into their own hands. At the other end of the spectrum, excessive positive liberty might manifest itself through a state bureaucracy arrogating too much power into its own hands to the detriment of people's wishes. Indeed, with the advent of modern digital technologies, they can even attempt to control how people should behave in private settings. Evidently, whenever there is an excessive preference for a particular liberty, whether positive or negative, people's liberties and rights suffer as a consequence.

[100] Arguably, the Rohingya refugee situation is a case where some blame must go to Myanmar's majoritarian establishment, since its leaders have not criticized the actions taken by the country's military establishment.

Attempting to Force-Fit New Root Elements
in the Spaces Belonging to GN Liberty
and Commercial-Objective

Since the model is arrived at by the doubling of functional spaces, people may mistakenly think that a *root-like* structure might be present in the bottom left space of sovereignty and commerce levels. To be clear, this would be tantamount to force-fitting *root* elements within GN liberty space and the commercial-objective space (refer to Figure 15 and Figure 2 respectively). Let us see why this cannot be the case.

Although the third level of sovereignty is created by carrying over the spaces created by the Golden Rules at the first two levels, the logic needed to interpret the sovereignty space is rather different from the Golden Rules. This is principally because Golden Rules make sense only when the root element is considered to be an independent agent capable of taking voluntary action. This core assumption no longer holds at the third level of sovereignty. If there had been such a volitional element within sovereignty, it would be present at the GN liberty space, where it would be capable of existing on a stand-alone basis in the model (refer to Figure 15). However, GN liberty comes into existence only along with the other three sovereign-liberties. Therefore, it cannot be deemed to be a stand-alone element.

From a more practical perspective, if GN liberty space is thought of as a root element, it could lead to several drawbacks in the liberty of individuals. To start with, IN liberty space (Judiciary) might be reduced to defending people's rights only against the overreach of the IP liberty space (Executive), since the root represented by GN liberty space (Legislature) might have a freer hand to abrogate an individual's liberties.[101] Such an interpretation does not make sense and is sure to be misused in many parts of the world.[102]

When we move to the next level of the model's buildup, which takes us to the commercial spaces of the model, there seems to be a need to assume the existence of a pseudo-root element within the model, namely the commercial-objective (refer to Figure 2). However, it is vitally important to recognize that this pseudo-root is only a subsidiary of the original root element since it exists solely to serve the interests of the original root. This understanding is critical when we move to the Stage-IV level, since the space of pseudo-root gets occupied by the commercial organization (refer to Figure 6), which cannot be treated at par with individuals.

Moreover, once the model has been completely built up, the Stage-III model itself can be treated as a new root element that becomes active at the next level of activity. For instance, this understanding of the model

---

[101] If a Legislature overrules the Judiciary on some structural matter of individual privacy, it means that the country is stuck at Stage-II when it comes to privacy violations, even if it has a veneer of democracy (perhaps majoritarian in character). That said, the typical Stage-II system will respect people's private spaces to a great extent, for most of its rights violations tend to be related to the public or regulatory space. If private spaces are being interfered with in an unrestrained manner, it is more a sign of a Stage-II system that has devolved down to a tyrannical system. In the present world, perhaps only the North Korean regime meets this definition.

[102] It is also possible to quote Montesquieu to bolster this particular point: *"When the legislature and executive powers are united in the same person, or in the same body of magistrates, there can be no liberty; because apprehensions may arise, lest the same monarch or senate should enact tyrannical laws, to execute them in a tyrannical manner."* After all, it was only a little while earlier that Louis XIV had declared, "I am the state." Some vestiges of this idea that the king or queen is the sovereign, and the people mere subjects, can still be found in the proceedings of the British system, which still runs the risk of being classified as a benevolent Stage-II system (it lacks a written Constitution capable of ensuring non-majoritarian results). To be clear, the successful presence of democracy implies that it is better thought of as a *de facto* Stage-III system. Moreover, apart from federations, at present there is no foolproof way in which to implement a non-majoritarian Bicameral Legislature, especially if the existing system is already a successful democracy.

itself as a new root element is pertinent at the Stage-IV level.[103] As part of avoiding *mala fide* disputes, the commercial organizations of Stage-IV must not hurt both the root elements, namely the original root of individual liberty and the new root represented by the laws of the sovereign state (voluntarily created by the people).[104]

Attempting to Force-Fit the Fundamental Protection of Private Spaces as Implying Something More than the Human Conscience Right

There are a number of areas in the modern world that threaten people's privacy. But not all such claims can be defended by invoking the Human Conscience Right per se. In particular, it should be made clear that the *fundamental protection of private spaces* in the model is derived entirely from the Human Conscience Right. Therefore, the privacy norm of the model can defend only the privacy claims of a relatively narrow subset of the contested areas.

For instance, if someone wished to compel people to do something against their will, that would be an invasion of privacy since it would require an invasion of the regulatory spaces present within the brain. Similarly, if someone wished to access the memories or feelings of another person without that person's voluntary cooperation, it would also violate privacy. At the other end of the spectrum, automated surveillance of public spaces like streets and airports does not seem to impinge on the Human Conscience Right. Indeed, such surveillance in the public interest is already a part and parcel of modern life.

---

[103] Similarly, when it comes to the space of foreign affairs, the Golden Rules relevant at the private space of people become valid once more, only this time the Rules must be made to make sense at the level of nations. We have summarized this situation in Table 6.

[104] Chapter One gave a formulation of the Golden Rule in the commercial context. This root-level analysis perhaps offers a structural rationale for the same.

That said, there are some privacy advocates who argue that public surveillance should not be used to identify individual people based on their known, unique attributes. However, if we rely on the logic of the model alone, such an identification would become a privacy violation only in the event that the information from the surveillance is used to influence the individual in any undue targeted manner, such that it interferes with their unfettered human conscience.[105] Not that the correct position is to allow the automatic identification of people from their unique attributes—rather, this is an area where the model, on its own, cannot give an answer. Instead, the answer must come from the real values of the people.[106] The model does its part by explicitly requiring that legislations convey this sentiment of the people.

However, there are other areas where people's privacy limits seem more likely to be infringed. Take the case of automated surveillance of cyberspace communications. Even if legislators want to allow some limited automated surveillance in this area, they have to contend with the fact that the model also allows for important privacy positions to be incorporated via a UDHR-like approach in the Constitution. For instance, UDHR explicitly includes within it the protection of private correspondence. If there is a tension between the legislators—who are short of the super-majority required for Constitutional Amendments—and the rights already enshrined in the Constitution, it is an area that the Supreme Court can weigh in on.

---

[105] In this connection, it must be mentioned that storing information collected from people's private spaces, like their properties and homes, should be disallowed. Moreover, in case some commercial organization has data of a substantial fraction of the citizens, there should be governmental regulations on the accessibility of that data to the organization's employees. Measures like these are necessary to protect citizens from bad actors present in large organizations and government departments.

[106] For instance, there can be preprogrammed analysis of data to spot potential problem trends before they reach full fruition, based on which follow-on approvals can be sought from the higher Judiciary for a deeper, manually supervised analysis.

2. MISINTERPRETATIONS RELATED
TO CHAPTER SIX

The following misinterpretations need to be avoided in relation to Chapter Six:

1. Force-fitting the model as having absolutely no possibility for customization.
2. Force-fitting all democracies as automatically compliant with the model's Stage-III norms.

Attempting to Force-Fit the Model as
Having Absolutely No Possibility for Customization

Perhaps the best example of a guideline within the model, which makes changes to the model difficult, is the *non-adversarial* imperative. If we try to adhere to this guideline that no higher level can be adversarial toward the lower-level spaces, we quickly realize there are not that many ways in which the model can be built up. However, there are many (important) areas in the model where different customizations may be considered.

Let us examine two such areas here to give a rough indication of their breadth. First, the methods by which people choose representatives to the two houses of Legislature can be customized to suit the context of a given country. For instance, this work suggests the plurality method for the first house and proportional vote-share representation for the second house. Needless to say, alternative approaches are possible in both areas. A prominent example is federal systems since, there, the second house tends to represent the constituent states. Moreover, the vote-share representation suggested for the second house has a number of problems, which suggests it needs a more thoughtful approach.[107]

Second, the model can differ on the method by which Justices are appointed to the Supreme Court. While the US prefers a top-down style where the nomination is made by the president, the Indian system is a bottom-up approach where the nominations are made via procedures followed by the Supreme Court. Obviously, both approaches have checks and balances which ensure that the initial power of nomination does not become a *fait accompli*.

Of course, the two Supreme Courts also differ from each other on a number of other parameters, like the number of Justices that are present on the Court, their retirement protocols, etc. Obviously, since Justices of the US Supreme Court do not have a retirement age, their nominations must come from some outside source. Also, a court with a lower number of Justices will naturally tend to focus their attention on fewer (but more important) cases, which would suggest that such a court would be

[107] The vote-share representation will only work as long as the largest party gets less than 50 percent of the vote-share. In case the dominant faction gets more votes than the preset threshold, there is the option of filling the Unification House with those who finish as runner-up to those in the Administrative House. This may seem like an unusual idea, but something like this is required to ensure that the democratic Stage-III system, especially in non-federal settings, cannot devolve into a majoritarian system. In the setting proposed above, it is likely the dominant factions will try to get as close to the threshold vote share as possible, but no further, as that will wind up hurting their power. It seems this approach is liable to the criticism that it may strengthen political polarization instead of building a moderate center, but the alternative of majoritarian electoral power seems worse. Recall also that the model expects democratic systems to have multi-party politics with more than just two parties, and in such situations, severe polarization would be more difficult to achieve. Obviously, since this proposal is unlikely to get implemented in those countries where the current dominant factions think they have a good chance to get more than 50 percent vote-share (it might be difficult to implement in other geographies as well), we should keep our minds open for more nuanced proposals in this area.

closer to an implementation of the Constitutional Court than the united Supreme Court.[108]

There are many more examples where powerful customizations can be made to the model. It may be added here that the most important driver behind these customizations would be the need to make the model more agreeable to the local context, which would in turn be derived from the country's unique historical experiences.

Attempting to Force-Fit All Existing Democracies as Automatically Compliant with Model's Stage-III

Although this work is clearly based on achieving at least the Stage-III level of the Rights model, it would be a misinterpretation to say that this work supports all existing democracies in the world. This is because some of them have problems in dealing with things like the private space and majoritarian vote-share.

The first problem of having to protect the private space can be tackled to some extent by having an effective Judiciary, since the associated rule-of-law will automatically address this area. However, the latter problem of majoritarian-rule cannot be solved merely by having an effective Judiciary, since its rule-of-law is liable to get compromised if there is excessive pressure exerted by a faction with majoritarian vote-share. Therefore, solving the latter problem will require a Constitutional structure where majoritarian vote-share becomes a relatively rare occurrence.

---

[108] However, it is not clear whether having a dedicated Constitutional Court is necessarily better than having a united Supreme Court. Just to be clear, as shown in Figure 20a and Figure 4, the Constitutional Court is to the Supreme Court as the Unification House is to the Bicameral Legislature. Incidentally, if the traditional rule of law is understood as everyone (including the government) having to obey the established laws, it would be anchored by Constitution within the Constitutional Court.

In other words, if democracies are to be considered as fully in line with what is proposed in the model, they must achieve at least the self-correcting nonviolent democracy position (explained in Chapter One). Although a healthy implementation of the four sovereign-liberties will ensure that the Judiciary can protect the private space from an overzealous Executive, implementation of unification-regulators will be required to eliminate the problem of majoritarian-rule.

If a democracy with a majoritarian faction is consistently providing rule-of-law for all its citizens, it may have to be considered as lying within the model's Stage-III. However, such a majoritarian situation would imply the country has not yet optimized the implementation of unification-regulators.

3. MISINTERPRETATIONS RELATED
TO CHAPTER SEVEN

Some of the misinterpretations to avoid in relation to Chapter Seven can be listed as follows:

1. Force-fitting the model as disallowing the practice of taxing public servant salaries.
2. Force-fitting the model as avoiding market forces in the infrastructure space.
3. Force-fitting UBI as an immediate requirement.
4. Force-fitting the model as the solution for energy and climate resilience.
5. Force-fitting the model as suggesting some specific environmental approach or solution.

Attempting to Force-Fit the
Model as Disallowing the Practice of
Taxing Public Servant Salaries

Although the model treats all expenses related to public servants as a *cost* borne by the people, this should not be interpreted to mean that the public servant salaries are *purely* an expense, such that it becomes, by definition, untaxable.

In particular, it is only in the historical Stage-II cases where agricultural surplus was the *sole* source of energy surplus that the taxes paid by public servants can be considered as a round-tripping of the funds taxed from ordinary citizens. In the current context of fossil fuels, it makes perfect sense to treat all productive citizens under an equal tax umbrella. After all, fossil fuels cannot be made available exclusively by the efforts put in by the private sector. Rather, bringing these fuels online requires some efforts to be put in by the public servants as well.

Not just that, if the high-EROI (Energy Return on Energy Invested) areas of Stage-IV systems can be unlocked by publicly funded research and development activities, the fact that all the original energy used to come exclusively from the efforts of ordinary citizens, or the private sector, would become even less important than in the current fossil fuels era. While bringing fossil fuels online required only some basic regulations and infrastructure to be put in place by public servants, bringing Stage-IV-level, high-EROI sources online would require a far more pro-active approach to planning by the public servants. Therefore, it is arguable that the unlocking of high-EROI areas should trigger a position where the public servant salaries are considered to be as equally productive as the efforts put in by the private-sector participants.

That said, this still would not mean that we can treat the productivity of the two sectors as equal in terms of relative importance to the nation. They are to be treated on a similar footing only with regard to taxation. If the nation's economy shrinks over a prolonged period, it will become critical to know what constitutes the nation's foundation and what represents the upper floors built on top of that foundation.

Fortunately, in the absence of such a severe economic climate, it would certainly be counter-productive to treat public servant salaries purely as an expense. Such an approach would probably mean that we cannot direct - sufficient efforts through the public space. As a consequence, the concerned economy would not flourish as much as it would have otherwise.

Attempting to Force-Fit the Model as
Keeping the Infrastructure Space Insulated from Market Forces

It may be possible to position Hayek as disagreeing with the model's infrastructure focus, for according to him, *"The curious task of economics is to demonstrate to men how little they really know about what they imagine they can design."* In order to defend the model against Hayek's design charge, it may be noted that this work is vital for clarifying the quasi-logical structure that exists within rights. Persisting with the design argument beyond a point will lead to the questionable position that, since human rights is a design, it should be done away with. Presumably, this would be an outcome unacceptable to most people.

Moreover, there is little doubt Hayek's real position was that the price discovery mechanism of markets should not be tampered with, which is a position this work certainly agrees with, even in the infrastructure areas. If an organization is part of the infrastructure area, it is not an excuse to be exempted from the disciplined performance that the market forces automatically enforce. Having said that, if Stage-IV systems want to maintain or restore the planet's natural ecology as part of the infrastructure initiative, it is not immediately obvious how the market forces can be used in the domain.

At the same time, it may also be noted that it was Germany's feed-in tariffs that helped drive the solar power costs lower in the early days of solar power. Thus, the right public policy in the infrastructure area can drive market efficiencies in a big way. Of course, when it comes to high-tech areas like a high-EROI generation, space debris removal, battery technology, and energy diversity planning, only a few countries have the capacity to take up these areas as part of their infrastructure initiative.

Attempting to Force-Fit UBI as an Immediate Requirement

UBI has been mentioned in this work primarily for the sake of theoretical completeness, and it is certainly not meant for an immediate implementation. There are some big problems to be solved first before a UBI can even be considered, at least if the UBI implementation is to be stable over a relatively long period of time, like a human life span.

First, the concerned country must have already reached, or be very near to reaching, a high-EROI energy supply system that is not based on fossil fuels. Otherwise, the stability of a UBI system in most nations will be far lower than a similar system that might be implemented within oil-exporting countries. In both cases, the underlying economic and resource situation is such that the payout will have to be stopped within a relatively short period of time. If not, the economy and currency will collapse, or the resource base will get exhausted.

Moreover, if there is a UBI system, its existence is bound to create a strong temptation for politicians to promise an increase of the payout, without much thought to whether such an increase can be maintained. For instance, changes to the existing welfare system require careful planning and execution. By contrast, changes to UBI might appear effortless to deliver in the short term. Therefore, if there is to be a stable UBI system, any change to it must necessarily have a higher threshold than the typical legislative enactments or budgetary allocations.

Perhaps it can be arranged that any change to UBI will require a Constitutional procedure with a super majority or even a separate Constitutional amendment. After all, getting to provide UBI implies the Stage-IV-level EROI supply has already been achieved, and in such a situation, it is absolutely essential that the concerned countries set up many other complementary systems within their Constitution in order to protect the environment.

As an aside, although UBI appears to be a good combination of elements in both the public space (the payment) and the private space (how the amount is spent by the citizen), direct welfare measures around food, water, and shelter may always remain more important.

Attempting to Force-Fit the
Model as the Solution for Energy and
Climate Resilience

It is likely that the defining struggle of our times will be in the areas of energy and climate resilience. Possibly, the greatest benefit (or relief) to humanity will come from those who can effectively contribute in these areas. It seems inevitable that if the solutions to these areas are to be effective, they will converge on the same solution—clean energy with high EROI. Developing better crop variety may also be an effective approach. Thus, people working on the technologies for addressing these concerns have the best shot at contributing most effectively.

Unfortunately, as of now, the model cannot directly address the twin issues of energy and climate resilience. It can only say that the environmental threats discussed in relation to external stability make it possible to address the two areas. For instance, reducing the risk of *energy shortages* and *solar storms* are closely connected with the issue of *energy resilience*.[109]

However, since acting on the environmental threats can only be done by the power-regulators, the initiative should come from them. If the model itself is to be seen as the solution, then it should have explicitly identified these areas for mandatory action, which it cannot do, for that would be like forcibly hijacking the power that belongs to the people. Therefore, the matter must be decided by the people and their representatives.

The model only suggests, via the discussion on environmental threats, that the two areas of energy and climate resilience should be accorded high priority, ideally through the medium made possible by an active Restraint-function. However, since there are other areas that can also legitimately qualify as environmental threats, like food and water security and agricultural biodiversity, the two areas of energy and climate resilience will have to compete for funds, along with all other areas.

---

[109] As far as a technological civilization is concerned, danger from solar storms (and associated coronal mass ejection) is far greater than the danger from asteroid impacts. Not only is the frequency of serious asteroid impacts rather low, but most of the larger asteroids have been mapped. By comparison, dangerous solar storms occur several times even within a human life span, and the most severe storms probably pack far more punch than our historic experience would indicate.

Attempting to Force-Fit the Model as
Suggesting Specific Solutions to Environmental Challenges

It is to be noted that the model can at most *flag* some areas as worthy of environmental action, like those identified in the external-stability discussion, but it cannot suggest specific *solutions* for those areas.

To drive home this point about the model being unable to specify the actual *solutions* to environmental challenges, we can discuss two areas— *population stabilization* and *energy constraints*. These two areas are connected with the lectures of Professor Albert Bartlett (who was an emeritus professor of physics at the University of Colorado at Boulder). Incidentally, exposure to his lecture was the initial inspiration for this work, coming as it did, immediately after the onset of the financial crisis of 2008.[110]

With regard to the first issue of *population stabilization*, although Professor Bartlett may have favored this due to environmental concerns, this model is not built with that objective.[111] However, if a country does decide to stabilize its population through legitimate democratic means, this model cannot automatically invalidate that approach, for it would be like automatically invalidating the concept of democracy itself. Such negations are possible only if the adopted measures violate some basic tenets of human rights.

---

[110] His concern is expressed in his lectures: "*The greatest shortcoming of the human race is our inability to understand the exponential function.*" Although this quote makes it seem as though exponential growth is hard to explain, it is actually so easy to explain that even school children can do it. Our real problem is that we have trouble internalizing the impact of exponential function with regard to time. Based on the unconscious model we have of the world around us, we expect things to remain largely as they are. But if we are in the midst of some unprecedented exponential change, it will completely upset that unconscious expectation, and such change can only be stopped (eventually) by natural environmental limits.

[111] Moreover, the UN projections are clear that the world population will stabilize in this century. Not just that, but there is a growing opinion among demographers that the UN projections err on the higher side. It is possible that the population will not only stabilize sooner, but it will decline sharply in most developed countries if there is no immigration into those countries.

For instance, there is fear that population control measures can be misused against minority groups, and if that turns out to be true, the model does automatically invalidate the concerned policy, for it insists all citizens have equal rights and dignity. Besides, it is now common knowledge that the best solution for stabilizing the population is to educate girls and ensure they enjoy the same freedom as their brothers. Surely all Rights-based models would align with that common-sense approach, but such models cannot actually suggest education as the specific means for population stabilization, for that might be outside their domain.

With regard to the second issue of *energy constraints*, it has been suggested in many knowledgeable circles that the exploitation of limited resources ought to be controlled by governments. The idea is that such control may be necessary to ensure that the world's finite resources are still available for the enjoyment of future generations. Although the model cannot advocate this particular approach, if it is done by legitimate means in a Constitutional democracy, it cannot be disallowed either.

However, it is unlikely that such top-down measures will get consistent democratic support, for if there are needy people at any given time, all the resources that can be made available will be made available.[112] Fortunately, there is an additional nuance that this model can introduce. In order to meet such *needs*, there is the option of creating the requisite *infrastructure*.[113] This option of public infrastructure can, if used well by

---

[112] The *needy* people being spoken about are mostly found in the poorer developing countries, such as those in Africa and the world's tropical areas where people have not yet achieved even the most basic necessities of life that are taken for granted in the developed countries.

[113] Research has shown that urban infrastructure requires fewer resources per person as the number of people present in the urban centers increase. The larger findings are summarized in Geoffrey West's book *Scale*. Moreover, Bricker and Ibbitson's *Empty Planet* sees urbanization as driving lower fertility rates.

governments, overcome environmental bottlenecks.[114] However, just as in the case of the girl-child education, this would be another case of the model being in alignment with a solution without actually suggesting it.

The above arguments on *population stabilization* and *energy constraints* may seem too specific to be applied in a general manner across all environmental challenges. Fortunately, there is another more generic argument which holds across all such challenges. It simply points out that models are not flexible enough to tackle problems outside their core domain. In other words, Rights-based modeling cannot suggest specific solutions to any problem, unless the solution is a structural feature of the model itself.

---

[114] This idea that the infrastructure space of the model can address the moral quandary posed by the seeming depletion of resources is interesting. But the idea itself is not new. In his magnum opus *The Wealth of Nations*, Adam Smith talks about the need for infrastructure in areas like banks, public works, education, etc. The notable modern addition to Smith's view on infrastructure may be that it is most important to look at the level of EROI that a nation's infrastructure can support. If it dips too low, or there are other risks to EROI, adequate investments must be made to ensure that the EROI level stays stable.

Part Three

SHORTCOMINGS
of
THE MODEL

9

Self-Correction
and
Monetary System

If the Stage-IV level of developed democracies is to be achieved, the organizational spaces must be developed properly. With that objective in mind, this chapter will attempt to clarify the model's position with regard to the Stage-IV developmental-regulators. Although we cannot precisely pin down developmental-regulation, we may analyze the organizational spaces (refer to Figure 6) by focusing on its two main areas—private and public spaces. Accordingly, this chapter will present an analysis of each area.

The first section looks at the private organizational spaces and suggests that a self-correcting force be enabled there. The second section looks at the public organizational spaces and suggests that a theory of the monetary system be developed there.

1. RULE-OF-LAW IN THE
PRIVATE ORGANIZATIONAL SPACE

Implementing an effective rule-of-law in the private organizational space may require us to set up an organizational paradigm that has some innate self-correction capacity. This position is explained below.

A. Intent Director and Self-Correction

Apart from ensuring that commercial organizations behave as per the established legal norms, Intent Directors must ensure that the organization does not come into conflict with the negative Golden Rule, albeit as applied in the organizational domain. At the very least, this implies that the rights of citizens must not be violated.

It must be emphasized here that this particular model, or some specific future version of it, cannot by itself provide the necessary level of understanding with regard to the Golden Rules or the rights of citizens. Instead, it is much more likely that such an understanding has to be evolved in a fashion similar to the way the criminal code evolved over a long period of time. Criminal law came into being based on people's complaints, which were gradually codified into a systematic canon. Similarly, the law for dealing with *mala fide* disputes will also come into being only gradually, principally based on the complaints filed by the affected people and organizations.

The Intent Director is likely the party responsible for filing such cases on behalf of the organization.[115] If society encourages this active watchdog activity inside organizations, organizations will have no option but to create some additional capacity at the level of Intent Directors, so as to ensure that they can mount an adequate legal defense in case any of their organizations' activities are challenged in the courts.

The expectation is that this will create self-correcting forces within the commercial sector, such that no organization is confident enough to initiate actions that might be in violation of the negative Golden Rule in the organizational domain.[116]

If there is a favorable verdict in a case brought in by an organization, the responsible Intent Directors and organization should enjoy some mandatory rewards as well. Perhaps the reward for the organization could include reductions in the taxes (up to some limit) that would otherwise have had to be paid in a default situation.[117] The good thing about this reward proposal is that even if only a few organizations take the Intent Director's watchdog role seriously, the commercial rule-of-law of the entire country can nevertheless be kept in good shape by those few organizations.

---

[115] Although most of the responsibilities of the Intent Director are meant for protecting the people from the overreach of organizations (mostly by ensuring that the existing laws are not violated), when their responsibilities are sought to be viewed purely at the organizational level, it may also explain why some rights cannot be waived by the right holder. Someone waiving their rights to be protected against slavery or torture would in effect be threatening the well-being of others in the community. Therefore, in such situations, the community (in the interest of all individuals) will demand a stop to such irresponsible rights waivers. Something similar needs to happen at the commercial organizational level as well. Irresponsible behavior of any organization, especially in relation to their interaction with individuals, must be spotted and called out by others in the commercial arena. This may go a long way in ensuring everyone's interest.

[116] If this is to be considered successful, it will have to prevent such occurrences as the subprime mortgages, large exposure to financial derivatives, student loans with no career prospects, etc.

[117] Keep in mind, this system is likely to be effectively implemented only in quasi-Stage-IV countries that already have a mature and capable Judiciary. In other words, Stage-III systems may need to implement other reforms first in order to build up the system's overall capacity.

In other words, although the law would allow it, it would not be necessary for every commercial organization to seek returns in the form of lower taxes from their Intent Directors. Moreover, if the appropriate tax incentives are in place at the organizational level, it is not only the Intent Director who will be interested. It would also encourage Equity Directors to participate. Indeed, Equity Directors might even actively seek to reduce the tax burden on their organizations by pointing out things that have to be corrected in the organizational sector—without any encouragement from the Intent Directors.

Needless to say, in case there is a verdict against an organization, the penalty should not fall on the Independent Directors of the losing organizations, but rather on the losing organization itself. The existence of such incentives will create some extra momentum in favor of self-correction in the organizational spaces. Eventually, the law might be sophisticated enough to deal with a great many of the *mala fide* cases on its own. Nonetheless, if this scenario does play out well, the role of the Intent Director will always remain essential for the health of the overall system.

Obviously, the above discussion around the responsibilities of Intent Directors has some experimental suggestions that could disrupt the current business-as-usual approach. Consequently, if an implementation is considered, it must be for some select demarcated areas, so that the feedback from the pilot implementations can be used to improve our approach in the area.

There is also the possibility that a special organizational charter can be given to those entities that want to perform watchdog activity. This might be similar to the accounting firms that are active today. If this works, it might lower the expectations put on the typical organizational board by the larger legal system.

B. Responsibilities of the Intent Directors

Following the above discussion on Intent Directors, we can summarize the key responsibilities of the Intent Directors as follows:

1. Veto any fresh initiative that could be construed as illegal or cheating
2. Ensure the organization can defend its activities in case it is challenged in court
3. Report any activity by other organizations that could be viewed as illegal or close to cheating
4. Encourage all organizations to have the wherewithal to defend their activities in court
5. Contribute to the society by constructively supporting the norms around dispute resolutions

While the first two points deal with the organization's own internal issues, the next two points deal with the activities of other organizations. Finally, the last point looks at supporting the system as a whole. Although the five points are mostly self-explanatory, the first point dealing with veto power requires a closer look.

It is fairly clear from the structure of the model that only the Equity and Intent Directors should be able to veto suggestions at the board level. Neither the Executive nor the Obligation Directors should have the veto power, for those positions are not as critical with regard to the organization's mission.

In addition, the Intent Director may have a role to play in the selection of Obligations Director. Perhaps Intent Directors can be expected to use their veto more often here than in any other area. After all, the existing position is to club the functions of Obligations Director and Intent Director into the Independent Director's role.

C. Regulation of Organizational Feedback

The above discussion on the responsibilities of Intent Directors is basically calling for feedback from organizations to be facilitated in the space of rule-of-law, just as feedback from organizations is allowed in the space of democratic-inputs. However, unlike with individuals, these two types of organizational feedback must be regulated differently.

Feedback from organizations in the area of rule-of-law is far more valuable than feedback from the same organizations in the democratic-inputs space. This is partly because an individual's feedback in the area of commercial disputes (i.e., rule-of-law) cannot possibly take into account all the minute details that would be privy to those operating within the more privileged setting of organizations. Therefore, it makes sense to take inputs from organizations in the area of Stage-IV rule-of-law. Basically, no other stakeholder in society will be able to provide those vital inputs.

On the other hand, since the Constitutional model gives sovereignty only to the people, an individual's feedback is the only feedback that matters in the area of democratic-inputs. This means that while organizational inputs in the area of democratic-inputs can certainly be given, it must be given only on publicly accessible forums, so that conflict of interest issues can be avoided.

This suggests that any lobbying done by commercial organizations should not have components of monetary value. Instead, lobbying should have only an information component, and the associated information should always be made available for the people's inspection in the public domain. Indeed, when information is publicly available, all interested agents can adjust their own inputs in the democratic-inputs space, provided they think the information is relevant.

Finally, it is notable that just as the Equity Director's permission is necessary to lodge a complaint with the rule-of-law regulators, the Intent Director's permission may be necessary to give feedback in the area of democratic-inputs.

2. RULE-OF-LAW IN THE PUBLIC ORGANIZATIONAL SPACE

Implementing an effective rule-of-law in the public organizational space may require us to develop a theory of the monetary system, along with the associated details of banking. In doing so, it seems we also need to address the area of *unavoidable* monopolies. This set of areas is examined next.

A. Special Case of the Monetary System

The two positive, sovereign-liberties, namely IP and GP liberties, assume that public servants have a monopoly in certain aspects of service delivery to the people. This monopoly in public service can be defended as necessary to achieve uniformity in policies in some unavoidable areas, like the fire protection system and the police system. Therefore, when there is a similar occurrence of monopoly at the commercial level, it is reasonable to expect that it will also be regulated by the Control- and Executive-functions.[118]

---

[118] If not, then citizens are being exposed to a potentially exploitative relationship from which they may have no recourse. If a complaint is filed with the Judiciary that there is compulsion or interference in the private space due to a commercial monopoly, it is hard to see how it can be redressed without the additional layer of regulation from IP and GP.

Obviously, the most recognizable monopoly at the commercial level is the nation's monetary system. Almost all commerce within a nation depends on it. In particular, it should be noted that if the Control-function regulates the monetary system, it will be a passive function, unlike today's interventionist central banks.

In particular, Control-function might just keep track of economic numbers and energy supplies as part of the Audit function shown in Table 4.2. After all, Ombudsman only attempts to resolve complaints that are activated by other agents, and Quality function's actions ought to be automatic when its passive quality thresholds are crossed.

Of course, to have such passive regulation, the monetary system has to be firmly tethered to the empirical world through parameters like commodities or energy availability. Setting up such a monetary system will require a deep understanding of several fields like economics, availability of resources in various countries, banking, the current situation in international finance, and other areas.[119]

Unfortunately, it is probably not possible for any one country to do a reform of this nature. Although the US can certainly take the lead, it will need the support of many countries. Therefore, it is likely that any change of this magnitude will have to be globally coordinated.[120]

---

[119] Crucially, following the 2008 crisis, it is clear that the current understanding of the monetary space is due for an overhaul. Although the financial system did not crash, the remedy that was applied—sovereign bailout for too-big-to-fail institutions—is greatly increasing the inequalities present in society, especially in the developed nations that were at the epicenter of the crisis. Since the financial sector was not sufficiently reformed following the crisis, the current system seems designed to take care of the richest, while ignoring the needs of all others.

[120] Notably, this reform of the monetary system is probably linked to the question of how security in the high seas can be arranged, so that global trade can continue. For instance, if the US dollar is no longer the major reserve currency, the world would probably have to pay the US to continue its role as the security provider. This is because the hardware that is necessary to do the security role cannot be created in anything less than a decade or two.

B. Banking System

Now that we have looked at the monetary system, let us move our attention to the banking system. To start with, while infra-organizations assay the role of public servants in the organizational space, banks may be understood as being limited to performing the role delegated by the monetary regulator present within the Control-function.

Control-function may enforce CHQ factors in the following manner with respect to banks:

1. Lending capacity of banks may correspond to cost and audit[121]
2. Adherence to regulatory guidelines may correspond to quality
3. Conflict of interest issues, like short-term profit-linked salaries,[122] may correspond to honesty[123]

Of course, like all normal companies, banks would also be subject to the regulation of Legislature and Judiciary. In particular, there should be legislations or amendments preventing banks from becoming too large, so that when they eventually fail due to poor lending decisions, despite sticking to the guidelines from Control-function, it will not cause a systemic crisis.

Moreover, since depositors should be considered as a bank's partners, they should probably be represented on the bank's board, via the position of

---

[121] Table 4.4 within this chapter will align this audit with the energy supplies available to the economy.

[122] Banking sector salaries probably should be benchmarked with that of the officials in the Control-function, and the profit margins probably should not be allowed to rise above some threshold.

[123] The crisis of 2008 appears to have been caused by conflict-of-interest issues (that were left unchecked), eventually translating into rampant speculation-related losses for financial institutions. It now appears these losses were then made good by the taxpayers without a comprehensive reform of the financial sector, with the result that many firms have again resumed their conflict-of-interest activities.

Obligations Director. Indeed, giving representation to the depositors might be more essential than giving representation to the bank's employees.

Central banks, which were meant to be independent institutions doing the Control-function's passive monetary role, have shown in the 2008 financial crisis that they can act discretionarily like an all-powerful Executive, especially if it required bailing out well-connected bankers in too-big-to-fail institutions.[124] It might help to start referring to these central banks as just monetary regulators since the current monetary system (an exponentially increasing debt-based system) does not actually require them to be bound by any empirical bank reserves.

If readers want to understand *exponential increase*, it can be compared to the doubling phenomena in the mathematics of compound interest. Alternatively, there is the story of a person asking for some grains of rice as a gift, with the squares of the chessboard being used to double the rice grains starting from a single rice grain. It turns out there is not enough rice in the entire world to fulfill such a request. Interested readers can easily confirm this in less than a minute via any spreadsheet software.

The existing system works as long as the system's debt is not too high, and there is a high EROI for the industry to fall back on. Once these factors stop being present, the assumption of exponentially increasing economic activity, based as it is on the assumption of exponentially increasing energy supplies, will stop working. In such a situation, the current central bank-based monetary system will fail.[125]

---

[124] Admittedly, it was necessary to defuse the crisis, but that rescue act should have been immediately followed by transparent advice to the government for sustainable reforms in the financial sector. Of course, ideally speaking, such advice should have been given much earlier, so the crisis itself could have been prevented.

[125] If so, it may help to note that the Bank of England was started in 1694 to enable the creation of a navy. Therefore, it is probably not a stretch to say that only those nations capable of maintaining an effective banking system over an extended period, say several decades, will be able to invest in, or bankroll, an effective navy.

The current system almost seems to treat the monopoly of the central banks as the IP function, with the banks as the GN functionaries. By contrast, the model suggests that while the banks may indeed be the GN functionaries, they are to be kept in check, not by the central bank in an IP function, but by the Control-functionaries represented by the CHQ of Table 4.4 (covered later in this chapter).

Nevertheless, in all likelihood, the system will persist despite its many flaws, until it enters yet another crisis it cannot resolve. Obviously, in a grave financial emergency, people will want to look at some alternatives. Unfortunately, such a contextually forced reform is likely to come too late for restoring many crucial aspects in the ecology.

C. Commercial Monopolies

It stands to reason that all commercial monopolies, by default, reduce the economic freedom of the people, at least in terms of the choices people have access to. Therefore, if organizations cross some transparently understood threshold of market power, perhaps linked to things like revenue or product share, the concerned organizations ought to be subjected to some additional regulations.

Although governments are prevented from interfering within organizations due to the need to maintain organizational autonomy, it is quite acceptable if governments intervene in markets at the level of antitrust activity. After all, such an antitrust intervention would entirely be driven by market metrics and not based on any internals of the organization per se.

For instance, antitrust enforcement makes sense only if the relevant market is large enough. In other words, market share monopolies in narrow niches may not attract any antitrust attention. For one thing, below some threshold of economic value, the cost of antitrust enforcement would become more than the benefits that could be passed on to the economy.

Also, if there is any change in the transparent metrics used to trigger the antitrust activity, there must be at least some fixed period of time during which organizations can voluntarily adjust their functioning so as to avoid becoming the target of government's antitrust enforcement. Incidentally, if something like this antitrust policy is implemented, it means that organizations above a certain market share would automatically be protected from unfriendly mergers and acquisitions.

However, some businesses may be *unavoidable* monopolies, in the sense that they may not be readily amenable to antitrust remedies. For instance, in some situations, avoiding monopolies might impose too high a cost on the overall economy, and as a result, it would reduce national competitiveness. The most prominent examples of these unavoidable monopolies in today's world may be the various utility and technology-based monopolies.

In the area of utilities, there is a need to avoid redundant infrastructure within a nation, say in the rail or power transmission sectors. In the area of technology, there might be a need for ensuring economies of scale in a business. Since the antitrust function cannot automatically end the monopoly power in the above cases, it can be argued that only companies in such unavoidable situations need to be called monopolies. In all other cases, they are either broken up by the antitrust regulator or are too small in size to be concerned about.

Crucially, there must be mechanisms for enforcing the decisions of the regulator over the unavoidable monopolies. After all, it is perfectly possible that monopolies may prove rather unwilling to comply with the directions coming from the Control-function.

If we look at the alternate scenario of banks, the banking regulator would simply withdraw the banking license, and the concerned bank would have no option but to cease operations. However, that bank-specific approach is simply not going to work with monopolies since the services rendered by some monopolies would be irreplaceable in the economy. Therefore, it is necessary to put in place some alternate, but equally compelling, compliance measures.[126]

D. Control-Function's Regulation of
Banks and Monopolies

Now that we have looked at the monetary system, banks, and monopolies, it is time to bring all these elements together. This is done in Table 4.4 since it shows the proposals regarding the banking system and monopolies in the CHQ factor format.

While Table 4.3 was an extrapolation from Table 4.1, Table 4.4 is an extrapolation from Table 4.2. However, unlike the Control regulators of Table 4.2, the Control regulators of Table 4.4 *do* have the power of termination over banks and boards of monopolies, at least far more power than is enjoyed by the Control regulators of Table 4.2 over the empowered-regulatory functionaries. This extra power is probably necessary to make it clear that banks and monopolies do not enjoy the same privileged status as the Legislature and the Executive-function.

---

[126] Some ideas toward this end are presented in the Scope of Monopolies discussion in the next chapter.

Table 4.4 Stage-IV Control-Function's Regulation of Banks and Monopolies		
Factors	Functional Area	Relevant Parameters
Cost	Audit of Energy Supplies and Economy; also, cost of banks (and monopolies?)	Ensure energy/monetary system and banking (and monopolies?) are effective
Quality	Recognize/retain banks and monopolies	Ensure minimum quality of banks and monopolies (i.e., no passive bias)
Honesty	Ombudsman for banks and monopolies	Ensure no active conflict of interest in the banks and monopoly space

As mentioned earlier in connection with banks, while the Cost factor looks at the energy supplies and the overall economy, the Quality factor looks at the quality parameters that can be mandatorily enforced. The Ombudsman space investigates active complaints made by people and other organizations.

When it comes to monopolies, an obvious Quality metric to focus on might be the profit margins. In a normal market situation, it should not be far removed from the typical industry number. Similarly, regarding the Honesty factor of monopolies, its higher salary figures probably should rise only high enough that it remains competitive with the rest of the marketplace.

It may also be noted here that while banks seem to require the full suite of CHQ to be regulated effectively, it is possible regulating monopolies may require only the HQ portion of the CHQ factors. After all, it would be hard to defend a government compensating monopolies for some of their costs.

It is not yet clear how this situation is to be understood. This seems to suggest that the regulation of banks and monopolies are to be done by two different regulators, with each being specialized in its own niche area. Obviously, this would be a different form of specialization within the Control-function when compared with Table 4.1 and Table 4.3, since the regulative specialization is to be split up in such a manner that it corresponds exactly to the three CHQ factors.

Of course, this specialization of Control regulators associated with Table 4.4 might not be dissimilar from the regulatory specialization already suggested for Table 4.2. However, banks and monopolies seem to represent only two of the four sovereign-liberties, namely the GN and IP liberties, respectively. In comparison, Table 4.2 deals with controlling the settings of the four sovereign-liberty regulators. It may be that regulators associated with the two missing sovereign-liberties, which are the two rule-of-law liberties of IN and GP, have to be discovered and delineated by following some other approaches.

10

Ambiguous Areas in the Model

There are many areas in the model where the current level of description is somewhat ambiguous and can be improved with some effort. Of course, it is rather unlikely that most of these areas can get fully resolved in terms of a logical structure, but that is no reason not to try. At the very least, some of these areas can be described at more depth than what is presently achieved in the model.

These are the *ambiguous areas* that will be addressed in this chapter:

1. Imprecise logical expression of the Rights
2. Scope of public servant functions
3. Scope of criminal justice system
4. Scope of developmental-regulation
5. Scope of monopolies
6. Responsibilities of the Control-function

7. Responsibilities of the Executive-function

8. Responsibilities of the Restraint-function

1. IMPRECISE LOGICAL EXPRESSION OF THE RIGHTS

Although the interrelationship among the Rights is constrained by the model's overall structure and the quotes, the exact logical structure of the Rights has not yet been made available, at least not in any rigorous formal fashion. This means the model is susceptible to misinterpretations, even in good faith.

This problem is unlikely to be resolved, for it is probably impossible to specify the entire model in terms of formal logic without abandoning its capacity to align with human values. At best, additional effort can be taken to clarify the most likely areas of misinterpretation, so as to minimize the potential problem.

Indeed, this appears to be a problem common to all works that are not strictly logical. Therefore, works in the governance area probably have a responsibility to assume as true something like Kant's idea of treating all humans as ends in themselves and not merely as means. Arguably, Kant's position may be a prerequisite for maximizing liberty and rights. An additional commitment to the Golden Rules will not hurt either. Hopefully, this set of assumptions will greatly reduce the potential for misinterpretations.

2. SCOPE OF PUBLIC SERVANT FUNCTIONS

To start with, it is not clear how public servants and regulatory functions are going to be staffed. Fortunately, unlike the issue of staffing, we may say something quite definite about the *priority* between the various regula-tors. Notably, *priority* here does not mean there is a reporting relationship between the two regulators. Instead, it just means the model considers some functions as more important with respect to the model's integrity. For example, the sequencing of Rights used to build the model suggests that the public space empowered-regulators have priority over their ana-logues in the organizational spaces.

However, clarifying the priority between the Stage-II- and Stage-III-level empowered-regulators (refer to Figure 8b) appears to be more complicated. Perhaps each of the four Stage-III empowered-regulators can be viewed as having *broader powers* than their respective Stage-II counterparts. But Stage-II empowered-regulators do the function that is more critical to the health of the root element. Obviously, this distinc-tion is less clear cut than the sequence-based priority described in the above paragraph.

Things become even less clear when we consider staffing the Stage-II- and Stage-III-level empowered-regulators. Perhaps, in keeping with the carefully limited priority accorded to the Stage-III empowered-regulator (i.e., broader powers), the regulatory personnel could be required to complete a period of time in the Stage-II regulatory function if they are to be eligible for selection into the Stage-III regulator. Obviously, this is only a suggestion and does not necessarily follow the structure of the model.

Not just that, while the suggestion seems easy enough to implement with respect to the Judiciary, it is not clear how to implement it with respect to the Control-function. After all, while the Stage-II Control-function is to be divided as per the CHQ factors, the Stage-III Control-function may instead be divided as per the four sovereign-liberties. Moreover, even if something like this is considered for implementation,[127] it can only be considered for the two rule-of-law regulators. Obviously, the staffing of Executive and Legislative regulators cannot be constrained in such a rigid fashion, for they must represent the freedom of the people in a far more flexible manner.

In addition, it is evident from Figure 20b that public servants can work in either domestic or foreign affairs. This work by itself cannot specify whether the government policy regarding the selection of public servants in the different domains is to involve a separate selection and training or whether governments should have a general selection and training module for everyone, especially at the entry level.

That said, there must be some procedures in place so that the selection is open to all age groups. After all, voluntary service cannot be barred for any age group, provided the retirement age has not passed and the concerned Quality parameters can be met. In the higher-age groups, this may require a separate selection procedure that looks more at the work experience of the personnel. In fact, prior work experience probably should be an important criterion even in the general selection process.

Also, perhaps slightly on a tangent, it can be argued that sportspersons representing a country are providing voluntary service demanded by the people. If so, it has not yet been specified in the model how such service is to be valued. Similarly, it can be argued that scientists are also doing a work

---

[127] Notably, the suggestion requires a far larger number of senior personnel at the level of a Stage-II regulator, when compared with similar personnel at the Stage-III regulator. Although the number of such personnel is indeed larger at the Stage-II level in the Judiciary, it is hard to say whether this will also be true with respect to the various Control-functions. Obviously, when we speak of staffing the regulators according to the model, we are only thinking of the senior decision-makers in these regulators and not the clerical personnel. Moreover, while some may want to point out that special qualifications should be necessary in the case of a few regulators (like the CHQ of banks and monopolies), that argument should be made in the case of every regulator.

demanded by the people, and it can be evaluated as per the CHQ norms. Incidentally, sportspersons and scientists perhaps lie on either side of the public servant in terms of the freedom they enjoy. While sportspersons have less freedom than public servants in terms of the type of work, scientists probably have more freedom than public servants. This is because the work of scientists can be based on unique research proposals, which then get funded by some interested agency.

The question of how the CHQ factors of public servants are to be measured is perhaps too involved to be answered completely. Nevertheless, since the Cost factor is relatively straightforward, we may take a look at the remaining two factors. With regard to the Honesty factor, what we can say at a minimum is that statutes (and associated rules) should consciously steer clear of creating situations where some bad apples in public service might be able to extort the citizens. For example, all fines levied should have a documentary trail, and it should be possible for citizens to complain to the Ombudsman and others. There can also be additional measures like periodic self-reporting of the assets held by the public servant's immediate family.

With regard to the Quality factor, we should examine whether it is possible to assess the performance level of individual public servants in an objective manner, purely based on the work they have completed in a given period. There are bound to be many good practices in this area that can be adopted based on the needs of a country. At the most basic level, this would involve simple things like checking whether the personnel is absent from the office premises too often. Unlike the Honesty factor, which needs to be triggered by some active complaint, Quality assessment is continuously active in the background, from the initial selection onward.

3. SCOPE OF THE CRIMINAL JUSTICE SYSTEM

It is arguable that the model should give more details with regard to the criminal justice system. After all, it has been identified as one of the most important areas of the model. The reason why the model is silent on more details in this area is that it cannot force-fit additional assumptions if those assumptions do not arise naturally from the theory of Rights distinctions. That being said, it is probably necessary to at least attempt to give more details in this area.

For starters, the police should be regulated by the CHQ factors of Table 4.1. Crucially, this differs from the regulatory restraints put on the Judiciary, for the Judiciary functionaries are regulated by the CHQ factors of Table 4.2. In fact, it seems likely that even the lower-level Judiciary will have to be regulated by the CHQ factors of Table 4.2, since their responsibilities differ substantially from that of the police. Police can be classified as public servants,[128] whereas the judicial functionaries ought to be considered as part of the Stage-II regulators. However, this probably does not apply to the clerical functions within the Judiciary, but that seems too detailed an argument to get into at this level of description.

This model does not venture to guess what aspects of the legal profession can be derived directly from the model, since that probably requires a great deal of specialist knowledge regarding the legal profession. At best, it can be said the modeling of the Judiciary ought to yield at least some broad characteristics, like the CHQ factors of the Control-function. Perhaps the distinction the model has already drawn between criminal

---

[128] In fact, police personnel belong to the class of public servants who should be given the highest priority, principally due to the philosophical justification they bring to the defense of tax collection. Other public servants who can be deemed to have a similarly high priority would include the likes of firefighters, medical first responders, tax personnel, etc.

and civil disputes is all that can be hoped for. After all, that particular distinction has already given scope for improving the functioning of the Judiciary in the organizational spaces. In particular, it is unclear whether the model will be able to cast any further light on the working of the Judiciary within the domain of the criminal justice system.[129]

However, that does not mean reforms in the criminal justice system are being disallowed by the model. All aspects that cannot be derived from the model can be treated as ad-hoc solutions, and those are susceptible to reforms all the time. For instance, the budget allocated to policing is an ad-hoc item that the model cannot have a view on, and therefore, it can easily be reformed. Indeed, in a theoretical scenario where there are absolutely no complaints from the citizens about their peers to the governmental authorities, the police staffing can be taken down to zero, but obviously, this scenario is unlikely to come about in reality.

The ideal level of policing is best understood from the level of complaints the system receives, both with respect to overaction and underaction from police. While such complaints ought to be a ground for terminating some police personnel, both at the Quality and Honesty levels of CHQ factors, they should also be used to gauge whether the staffing numbers are appropriate for an area. It is critical that the complaints of people be treated seriously and transparently. For instance, benchmarking of the nature and type of these complaints should be easily available to the public.

---

[129] At best, the model may be argued to have a more lenient attitude to crimes done by individuals, as opposed to crimes done by organized groups. After all, any organized criminal activity can be treated as a more direct challenge to the Constitutional order, whereas an individual folly is probably not a threat to the Constitution itself. Keep in mind, this argument may require additional assumptions to be made with regard to the model. Lest there be any misunderstanding, crimes involving bodily harm to others would have to be treated as seriously as possible, even if it is done by individuals (without the help of organized groups). Also, at the other end of the spectrum, any nonviolent protest activity done by organized groups in the public domain cannot be deemed as criminal.

4. SCOPE OF
DEVELOPMENTAL-REGULATION

Let us attempt to understand the developmental-regulation in terms of evolutionary stages present in Figure 7a. Basically, the level of despotism that is possible in a society drops sharply as the society progresses first from Stage-II to Stage-III, and then from Stage-III to Stage-IV.

The initial shift to Stage-III is characterized by a full implementation of the overall-regulators (implies an inclusion of people's democratic feedback), which reforms the authoritarian system that would have been prevalent at the Stage-II political level. However, as per the model, despite attaining the Stage-III level, the society would still suffer from chronic economic underdevelopment.

Fortunately, in some benign environmental settings, it should be possible to move from Stage-III to Stage-IV as well. As per the model, this developmental shift to Stage-IV will be characterized by a full implementation of developmental-regulators. Notably, such a Stage-IV system would retain the non-majoritarian feedback system that would have been implemented at the Stage-III political level.

The developmental shift to Stage-IV may have to ensure the four regulatory positions mentioned in Table 11.

These regulatory activities are also present to some extent at Stage-II and Stage-III, but the positions mentioned (e.g., antitrust measures, infra-organizations, etc.) become mature only with systems capable of some Stage-IV-level functioning. Notably, although the antitrust measures are put in the bucket of the Legislative-function, the actual enforcement (as per the norms laid down by the Legislature) might be done by the quality arm of the Control-function.

Table 11 Developmental-Regulation in the Model	
Empowered-Regulators	Required Regulation from the Regulator
Legislative-function	Apart from taxes, some antitrust measures must kick in once some threshold of market power is crossed
Executive-function	The Executive must take feedback from external experts and public servants, so as to plan investments in a better manner
Judicial-function	Governments cannot arbitrarily interfere at the level of individual, commercial organizations
Control-function	Infra-organizations cannot use their privileged relationship with government to earn higher-than-normal profits

Since we have already covered three of the four positions in Table 11 prior to this, we need to explain now only the position of the Executive-function. Basically, the Executive cannot be in a position where it listens to public servants and infra-organizations only. While those two stakeholders will have an in-depth understanding of the existing situation, they are also likely to have vested interests in protecting the status quo. Therefore, just as listening to no one before taking public infrastructure decisions would be economic despotism, listening only to a certain set of stakeholders will also be a form of economic despotism. This does not necessarily mean the Executive must bring in people who are not from the pool of public servants. That would depend on the Constitutional provisions set up by the Legislature.

5. SCOPE OF MONOPOLIES

While it is competitive bidding for government contracts that increases the operational efficiency of infra-organizations, in the case of *monopolies* that cannot be broken up by antitrust laws (due to unavoidable market reasons), increases in efficiency must be brought about in a different way.

For instance, there could be a transparent market incentive for monopolies to both lower the costs and increase the service quality. This would be under the supervision of the Control-function.[130] If they are successful in meeting some preset targets, they can be rewarded proportionally by neutral market mechanisms, which operate under statutory and transparent regulatory limits. In other words, discretionary actions from regulatory officials should not be able to interfere with the reward mechanism.

However, if the monopolies cannot maintain their service quality above some minimum level, their license should be liable to be transferred to some new operator in a transparent bidding process similar to the infrastructural contracts. The new operator has to work with the existing organization since the equity of existing shareholders cannot be wiped out.[131] However, the new operator would have complete managerial independence for effecting the desired improvements within the old organization. Since the employees of the monopoly must work under

---

[130] Moreover, since other market participants will always be able to complain to the Ombudsman whenever the monopoly launches new services, it effectively means monopolies always need permission to launch new services. Clearly, such a regulatory burden on the monopoly enables other organizations to more successfully disrupt its functioning. As far as this model is concerned, monopolies should exist only in those cases where there are some unavoidable reasons for them to exist, and this can only be evidenced by their staying power in the marketplace, despite being hamstrung in various ways.

[131] The original equity holders can opt to continue to stay invested in the business, and thus, participate in any subsequent gains or losses in market capitalization. It is just that they can no longer nominate the Equity Directors, since that role will be taken up by the operator chosen by the regulators. Obviously, this would qualify as a sort of board reconstitution, and thus, it ought to be done only to mitigate some systemic problems or to deal with serious frauds.

the direction of the private sector managerial expertise—who take up a position similar to that of the original entrepreneur representing both Equity and Executive Directors—they must also be thought of as private sector employees and not as public servants.

The operator who is given charge of the monopoly does not own the business but instead operates it for a fixed period of time (probably not substantially longer than most Constitutional appointments) during which appropriate market-linked compensation can be given, of the sort mentioned above. Since there is a possibility that an appointed operator (need not own equity) will deliberately reduce the profits of the organization so as to get results that inflate the compensation given to the operator, one of the compensation criteria could be the maintenance of the profit margin above some threshold. If this minimum profit threshold is not high enough, there is a danger that the government will have to fund some capital-intensive projects necessary for the monopoly to keep functioning, which should ideally be avoided.

There may also be an expectation that the license for operating the monopoly will be renewed in the operator's favor as long as the quality of service meets expectations. Thus, if the Control-function decides to change the operator for some reason,[132] the decision must be defendable as per the law and the agreed-upon contract conditions, failing which the decision can be challenged in the courts by the operator (but probably not by anyone else). Although it might be difficult to reinstate an operator who has lost the faith of the Control-function, it should be possible for the operator to get compensated for any unanticipated termination.

---

[132] Control-function has the option of placing one of its nominees as an Intent Director on the board. Indeed, it is also possible all Independent Directors are nominated by some procedure that is outside the direct control of both the Control-function and the selected operator group.

If the above position on new operators being brought in to run the monopolies is unacceptable (or insufficient) for some reason, an alternative position can also be considered. It could be mandated that all monopolies will only have minority shareholders, such that no one holds shares above a threshold, and this threshold could be lower than 50 percent. This may make it easier for the rest of the board to implement the decisions of the regulator, even if there is some reluctance from Equity Directors representing the larger minority shareholders.[133]

Both the position of the new operator and the elimination of majority shareholding underline the fact that the government should not get involved in the actual running of the monopolies. Instead, government should focus only on monitoring the outcomes in the marketplace for ordinary customers, so monopolies can be held accountable if they fail to meet people's expectations, or worse, take undue advantage of their privileged market position.

Obviously, these are still tentative ideas and may be modified in future versions of the work. However, the basic imperative that the model cannot back away from is that in the event that a monopoly is unwilling (or too slow) to comply with regulations for some reason, there must be mechanisms for enforcing those decisions.

It helps that the commercial organization is an artificial construct created by the people, and when it comes to an unusual area like that of unavoidable monopolies, normal arguments of private property cannot

---

[133] It is important to ensure the equity holders receive the correct market compensation in the event of such a transaction. This will ensure people are not shortchanged for their past efforts. Besides, any majority shareholder in a company that became important enough to be considered as a monopoly will probably be able to contribute effectively in the marketplace through more efforts. Therefore, it is very much in the interest of the concerned country to enable a situation where such people can contribute again. And, due to the rewards involved, newcomers in the marketplace will be just as strongly motivated.

be pressed beyond a point. In many cases, but especially in the case of perceived systemic threats, people can add special provisions to the working of commercial organizations.

6. RESPONSIBILITIES OF THE CONTROL-FUNCTION

To better understand the Control-function, let us compare it with the other rule-of-law regulator, which is the Judiciary. To start with, both the rule-of-law regulators (at the Stage-II level) are meant only to regulate the functional space lying adjacent to them. However, although the Stage-II Judiciary is limited to regulating only the space next to it, the Judiciary's domain is large enough to include all the people in the country. In comparison, Stage-II Control's domain includes only voluntary public servants, which certainly exempts most of the citizens from its purview. This suggests that the Judiciary function ought to be considered as more powerful than the Control-function.[134]

Moreover, a similar argument can be made at the level of Stage-III as well—that the Constitutional Court is more powerful than the Stage-III Control-function, since the latter's powers may not extend to the domain of the Unification House and the Constitutional Court. Of course, the powers of the Stage-III Control-function can be viewed as broader than the powers of the Stage-II Control-function, since the former can regulate the transparent settings of the Stage-II empowered-regulators.[135]

---

[134] Although this comparison with the Judiciary suggests the Control-function is weaker, it also means that setting up the Control-function ought to be considered a higher priority than the services rendered by most public servants.

[135] Alternately, we can say that Stage-III Control-function is meant to ensure the commercial organizations do not get to interfere in the Stage-II regulatory spaces. After all, commercial organizations are bound to have some interests that diverge from that of the people, given that market pressures force companies to focus on the short term.

We can also examine the two rule-of-law regulators for the commonality they have with each other. For instance, since the Control-function is part of the rule-of-law along with the Judiciary, it suggests that it is an independent subject matter expert of some sort, perhaps similar to the Judiciary's expertise on law. Indeed, the functions of Audit, Retention, and Ombudsman require the CHQ regulator to have good subject matter expertise. Notably, the subject matter expertise in these areas may considerably eliminate the need for resorting to discretionary decisions, thus reducing the pressure on Legislature to specify all the granular details concerning the Control-function.

Control-function could also have responsibilities in areas other than those mentioned above, but such additional responsibilities are not easily defended. For instance, the concern is that by taking up additional responsibilities, the Control-function might be going beyond the suggested remit of the model, which is to regulate only the CHQ spaces (it automatically implies rule-of-transparency). Therefore, any additional proposal should be carefully scrutinized.

Since we are looking at the Control-function from the perspective of rule-of-law, it is worth mentioning here that if any infra-organization deliberately breaks some key norms that are sought to be guarded by the Control-function, it would have to be treated as a *mala fide* violation.

Finally, as envisaged in Table 4.2, the Stage-III Control-function can regulate only the transparent settings of Stage-II regulators. This means that the settings of other Stage-III regulators cannot be brought under the ambit of the Stage-III Control-function, at least not without adding more features onto the model, which may not be warranted. The set of Stage-III regulators exempt from the supervision of Stage-III Control-function cannot be considered as small since it would include the likes of the Unification House, Constitutional Court, head of government, Restraint-function, and the Stage-III Control-function itself.[136]

Perhaps the Legislature can think of some alternate means by which to regulate the CHQ factors of the functionaries present in the Stage-III regulators. However, as of now, such measures would be outside the model's structure and would have to be evaluated according to the various practical positions present in each country's Constitution.

7. RESPONSIBILITIES OF THE EXECUTIVE-FUNCTION

Notably, the model does not see any scope for a judicial review of the Executive decisions, except where the Executive decisions infringe on the rights of the citizens or violate the established laws. Obviously, this assumes a situation where the Stage-III CHQ over the Executive-function, as envisaged in Table 4.2, has already been effectively implemented. In addition, Executive-functionaries can be drawn from a wide pool composed of all qualified citizens, rather than from a small pool of the CHQ-based public servants.

Executive-function regulates the IP liberty of public servants and the infra-organizations. In both cases, Executive-function cannot interfere in the functioning of the respective Control-function, and it is mostly limited to working with the public servants and infra-organizations that the Control-function has approved. Admittedly, Legislature can give the Executive the freedom to bring in a few people from outside the small pool of public servants if it is necessary to perform the task at hand in a better

---

[136] Arguably, the head of government and Restraint-function fall under a separate category, since it may make more sense for them to be impeached by the Legislature.

manner.[137] However, it is more debatable whether this freedom should also extend to bringing normal, commercial organizations into the area of Executive discretion.

It appears as though the discretionary decisions of the Executive-function—especially with regard to the investments that are meant to keep the economy on a productive footing (ODSI approach)—can primarily be understood as public infrastructure projects. To be clear, the infra-organizations that work on these projects will execute it as per the directions of their own boards while meeting all the contractual obligations set out by the Executive. However, while failure to meet the expectations of Control-function is potentially a *mala fide* offense, failure to meet the expectations set out by the Executive may not be so serious.

Theoretically speaking, it can be suggested that the infrastructural decisions of the Executive should be guided by at least two imperatives—increasing the freedom of individuals (Mandela's quote) and increasing the energy availability within the nation. If these two imperatives are ever in opposition to each other, it is freedom that should get the priority. For instance, the underlying tension may be between increasing the energy availability in the nation and ensuring that the ecological aspects are not harmed (necessary to sustain individual freedom in the long run). In such a scenario, it is the environment which should get the priority since that is more closely aligned with people's freedom.

---

[137] There is a related question of what happens if the head cannot get its nominees for the Executive-function through the confirmation process. Perhaps there should be some structural features that can only be accessed by those nominees who get through the confirmation process, as opposed to those who hold the charge in a temporary capacity prior to the confirmation. The ability to bring in people from outside the pool of public servants may be one of those features that can only be unlocked after getting through the confirmation process.

This is easy enough to say, but probably hard to achieve in practice—mostly because it is usually difficult to determine when the environment is being irreparably harmed. It may be recalled that this is largely the dilemma described in the last section of Chapter Seven as well.

8. RESPONSIBILITIES OF THE RESTRAINT-FUNCTION

To better understand the Restraint-function, it is instructive to look at its responsibilities through the lens of the Intent Director. As may be recalled, the responsibilities of the Intent Director are summarized in the last chapter. It basically deals with three distinct areas:

1. Own issues
2. Issues of others
3. System-level issues

In each of these three areas, the matter can be examined in terms of action and inaction. Accordingly, as shown in Table 12, we may imagine responsibilities of the Restraint-function along the same lines.

Table 12 Restraint-Function in terms of Action/Inaction	
Area of Action/Inaction	Description of Activity
Activity of Own Country	
Ensure Inaction	Veto violent action from the head (if it is not in self-defense)
Ensure Action	Insist on having some self-defense (deterrence) capacity
Activity of Other Countries	
Encourage Inaction	Strongly discourage violence (if not in self-defense)
Encourage Action	Encourage self-defense arrangements that bring stability
System-level Activity	
Ensure Inaction	Veto unilateral attempts to abrogate international agreements
Environmental	*Climate change, sea pollution, etc.*
Ensure Action	Support for international stability (global order)
Environmental	*Investments into high-EROI areas, natural carbon sinks, etc.*

While the first two rows represent *own issues*, the next two rows represent *issues of others*. The last set of rows represents *system-level issues*. Although action and inaction in the case of *own issues* require a firm commitment with regard to the outcome, the nature of the outcome cannot be similarly controlled in the case of *issues of others*. As a consequence, while we need to *ensure* activities when dealing with *own issues*,[138] we can only *encourage* activities when dealing with *issues of others*—for the locus of control is not with us.

---

[138] Take for instance the need to *ensure* some self-defense capacity. While the office *of National Security Advisor* (NSA) already exists in a few countries, the NSA must necessarily report to the head, but Restraint-function would be an independent Constitutional position capable of restraining the head in the area of foreign affairs.

Moreover, although Table 12 brings up environmental responsibility only in the last area of *system-level issues*, the environment can also be mentioned with respect to the earlier areas. The reason the environmental aspect was not explicitly mentioned in the earlier areas is because the environmental activity in the earlier areas seems to align more with the *action* part and only rarely with the *inaction* part. For instance, all nations must ensure a minimum level of environmental resilience for themselves and must also encourage the efforts of all other nations in the same direction. However, it seems unlikely that a nation must be dissuaded from taking environmental actions that would hurt other countries but not itself.

We can also look at Restraint-function from the economic side, which is an angle not directly addressed in Table 12. For example, although the discussion on external-stability clarified that Restraint-function is meant to maintain stability of the nation with respect to foreign and environmental threats, it is not clear whether it has the power to check economic development. This is especially so since economic development is the responsibility of power-regulators. Indeed, this probably sums up the environmental crisis facing the world. We are unable to decide what kind of environmental changes are necessary before it harms the immunity of the citizens with respect to their environment. As long as that vital assessment remains unclear, the final decision on the part of economic development will rest with the power-regulators.

On the whole, it seems likely that if Restraint-function is to have success, it needs to have at least some latent powers (immunities?) whereby it can indirectly influence the decisions taken by the head of government. These could include the power of nominating people for key Constitutional positions (like the Control and Trade functions), power over trade sanctions, power of approval over legislations, power of inviting a parliamentary faction to form the government, and more. This aspect of Restraint-function was not addressed earlier, since it potentially confuses the roles of Hohfeld's Power and Immunity. Obviously, more study is needed on this important matter.

Of course, to ensure that these latent powers are not misused, there should be a provision in the Constitution for impeaching the Restraint-function as well.

9. OTHER AREAS

Obviously, the discussions in this chapter have only scratched the surface of the respective areas. Many areas have not been included in the discussions because there is nothing substantial to add to what we already said. For instance, we have not added anything here to our earlier descriptions of the Bicameral Legislature and the Supreme Court.

While *ambiguous areas* are mostly areas where practical positions can conceivably be implemented within Constitutions, there are also some other problem areas where the Constitution alone may not be sufficient. As hinted at in the above discussion on Restraint-function, these would typically be situations where the environment is involved. Fortunately, an analytical work like this can attempt to discuss some of these areas. We investigate these areas in the next chapter.

11

Failure Points in the System

Although we have laid out the model in a fair amount of detail, there are still some unresolved tensions that are serious enough to cause failure of the system. Since the potential for such a systemic failure is too important to ignore, this chapter investigates some prominent failure points in the system. As we shall soon see, these failure points cannot be fully mitigated by the Rights-based model alone. It will require a contextual or practical approach to handle these failure points.

First, we examine *response areas* where effective mitigation responses have been tentatively identified. Second, we look at areas termed *unresolved tensions*, where the identification of appropriate mitigation action appears to be harder.

1. RESPONSE AREAS

When it comes to failure points in the system, there are at least two areas where we can mount relatively effective mitigation responses. Consequently, we may call these two areas *response areas*.

First of the two is the ability to focus our efforts on leverage points within the Constitutional model, so that the entire system benefits from tightly focused efforts within a small domain. The second response area is our ability to respond to the threat posed by fossil fuel-induced climate change. We discuss these two response areas below.

A. Focus Areas for Improving People's Liberty

Since there is a danger of expending effort without getting sufficient gains in return, it is necessary to identify the areas that are likely to produce the most effective improvement in people's liberty—in other words, the most improvement with the least effort.

As per the model, the three most promising areas appear to be these:

1. Rule-of-law in the sovereignty space
2. Rule-of-law in the organizational space
3. Democratic-inputs

These three areas are identified via our understanding of external- and internal-stability. To start with, external-stability (Figure 18) identifies the sovereignty space as the crucial balancing point (or fulcrum) within the model. Thereafter, internal-stability (Figure 19) identifies rule-of-law as the crucial balancing point within the above-identified sovereignty space.

The two remaining components in the sovereignty space are democratic-inputs (GN and IP liberties), and they are also important. Notably, since they are part of the sovereignty space, they influence the fulcrum of external-stability. In particular, democratic-inputs could be influential by limiting the potential downside scenarios for the system. This aspect of democratic-inputs has been explained in the discussion on internal-stability.

In contrast to the risk mitigation offered by democratic-inputs, rule-of-law components may offer some upsides to the system, at least in the current context where the Constitutional structure has not yet been fully understood. Admittedly, improvements in the rule-of-law area will not be easy to achieve, except perhaps with regard to commercial organizations and the Control-function. After all, the Judiciary has already gotten a lot of attention over the years.[139]

In external-stability, if we look beyond its fulcrum represented by the sovereignty space, there is also the *de facto–de jure* balance represented by the two weights in the balance. However, these two areas cannot be improved by conscious efforts, for they represent the whole system. While *de facto* forces depend on the people's private spaces, *de jure* forces depend on the procedural norms associated with the unification-regulators.

These are complex multifaceted areas, and they will only change slowly at roughly the pace of the larger society as it passes through various travails over time. For instance, the balance in external-stability depends on whether the *de facto* private space is amenable to *de jure* legal

---

[139] Obviously, this should not be taken to mean that the rule-of-law around the criminal justice system cannot be improved. As discussed earlier, reforms in the area of criminal justice are quite feasible, especially with regard to the functioning of police personnel. Indeed, the model probably calls for some reforms in the working of police personnel via the implementation of the Control-function.

forces. Basically, many qualities of freedom in the public space will only be decided by the people's values and not by any model.[140]

Of course, if we look beyond the *de facto–de jure* balance in external-stability, there is also the matter of environmental threats. Not surprisingly, that is also something outside of our deliberate control. At best, some basic precautions can be taken to avoid the more obvious threats, but achieving a system where there are no serious environmental threats is impossible.

Take climate change for instance. Even if carbon emissions in the atmosphere can be brought down to the pre-industrial levels, the planet's climate will keep changing based on other factors. Incidentally, it was one of these random changes 10,000 years or so ago that gave us our current period of an abnormally stable climate, which happened to be conducive enough for settled agriculture.

A Closer Look at the Model's Leverage Points

To identify the best leverage points for improving democracy, we need to use perspectives that capture the entire theoretical space occupied by the model. If the perspective does not capture the whole theoretical space of the model, we cannot be sure of its reliability for the analysis.

Although there are several such encapsulating perspectives in the model—Ambedkar's reform, Berlin's liberties, Mandela's freedoms, Hohfeld's analysis—none of these seems to give us the necessary leverage for improving the performance of the system. For instance, even though Ambedkar's reform (Figure 5) and Hohfeld's analysis (Figure 10) give a good sense of the overall structure of the model, they do not identify a narrow area for us to focus on.

---

[140] Had the US fully appreciated this limitation in effecting deliberate improvements, it might not have entered countries like Afghanistan, Iraq, etc. Obviously, this is also true of the earlier Vietnam situation.

Fortunately, Lincoln's quote shown in Figure 18 gives us a focus area for improving the system's performance. After all, the sovereignty space appears to be the fulcrum of the balance in external-stability. Not just that, but when we extend this fulcrum-based thinking to Figure 19, it identifies the rule-of-law components of IN and GP liberties as the areas to focus on. Thus, we may tentatively identify the Judiciary and Control-function as the primary leverage points for improving the performance of the whole system.

B. Mitigating Fossil Fuel-Induced Climate Change

Since climate change could trigger a collapse of the present agricultural system, which is potentially catastrophic enough to set us all the way back to a Stage-I system, it is necessary to at least attempt to identify the most effective mitigation measures—in other words, those approaches that may get the most improvement with the least effort.

With regard to mitigating climate change, while we should pay more attention to the efforts aimed at decreasing the yearly emission of greenhouse gases like carbon dioxide, the underlying problem is tied to the stock already present in the atmosphere, and if that is not removed, fossil fuel-induced climate change cannot be mitigated.

This problem of reducing the burden from historic emissions will require a drastic reduction in the cost of energy used as input in the process of carbon sequestration. Obviously, if we get a new, high-EROI source, it will be of great help in this direction. However, in the interim, we need to look at alternate mechanisms to remove the excess atmospheric carbon dioxide that has been built up over the years.

If we look at the current options, probably the most cost-effective way to sequester carbon is through reforestation (recovering degraded peatland might be even more effective). This is not to be confused with planting a few sapling varieties or artificial monocultures. In particular, it is reforestation in the tropical zone that will be effective in capturing carbon from the atmosphere,[141] but it would still take several decades to have a meaningful impact. Moreover, even if all of the planet's original forest cover is regained, it would still sequester only about twenty years of the current emissions.

To incentivize tropical reforestation (and peatland protection), Stage-IV countries can transfer some of their energy surplus (this implies a payment) to countries willing to grow their tropical forests. In fact, this possibility is a higher priority than the Stage-IV UBI suggested in this model because the harmful impact from climate change could easily make the Stage-IV system itself untenable.

Needless to say, this high priority accorded to ecological restoration will only be relevant in a practical sense if there is a strong Restraint-function, which is just not true as of now. Moreover, this priority assessment is also subject to tropical reforestation continuing to be the most cost-effective way to sequester carbon. Further, politicians of rich countries will be reluctant to hand over money taxed from the economy to poor countries with tropical forests, even if the intended impact is to save the planet's ecology and climate.

Fortunately, there is another way, one that does not need the Stage-IV-level energy surplus. We can simply impose a tax, for this payment

---

[141] As a bonus, reforestation will also help many threatened species to regain their fast-receding habitats. Indeed, tropical forests are the most biodiverse areas on the planet.

alone, on international air travel and cargo.[142] Since this asks the most profligate of individual emitters to fund the most cost-effective of carbon sequestration, it seems like a legitimate option.[143] Alternately, temperate forests also offer some incremental sequestration capacity at a lower rate.

However, in the event something like this comes through, countries with tropical forests cannot get complacent about the reliability of the income stream (energy transfer), because rich countries may discontinue the arrangement once they find a less-polluting means of air travel, or alternatively, more cost-effective sequestration technologies.

A Closer Look at the Danger Posed by Climate Change

There is a need to better appreciate the fact that climate change is truly dangerous to future human well-being. While most people know that predicting the weather several days in advance is hard (e.g., rains), modeling the climate is also a difficult problem for somewhat different reasons.

Unlike the weather, which can be predicted accurately only in the short term, climate is more influenced by stable macro variables, with the result that it has predictable yearly patterns. However, when some of these macro variables (like the Arctic Sea ice or ocean currents) change due to a gradual warming, the predictable climate patterns that we are used to can also change.

---

[142] Of course, countries that are mindful of their historic emissions (e.g., US, Europe, etc.) and oncoming vulnerabilities (e.g., India, China, etc.) can go further and tax domestic air travel and cargo as well. Obviously, taxes raised from domestic air transportation can be used to enhance the environmental resilience of the concerned country.

[143] Perhaps some planned migration from the countries with tropical forests to other countries can also be considered, provided the populations of the concerned countries are willing. After all, lower population may go some distance in reducing the deforestation pressures. For obvious reasons, this approach will be harder to actualize than an international air transportation tax. If so, it is possible deforestation pressures might also be reduced by channeling some of the funding into urban infrastructure.

Indeed, most climate models do not even take into account the possibility of some potential feedback loops,[144] because it would become quite impossible to predict what would happen. Therefore, while the gradual warming of the planet predicted by the current models is certainly to be feared, the latent potential for an even quicker change makes climate change extremely dangerous.

At the same time, there is a need for an educated restraint so that we may avoid exaggerations. First, putting a sudden stop to our current fossil fuel use is certainly not going to prevent the fossil fuel-induced climate change. Unless we have an effective way of removing the existing stock of emissions from the atmosphere, we cannot claim to be in a position to mitigate the threat of climate change.

Second, when viewed in terms of a human life span, climate change is a long, drawn-out process. It is probable that in the short term, we are going to see more extreme events like hurricanes, floods, droughts, heat waves, and forest fires. Developments like these certainly have the potential to cause massive migration waves. On a longer-term timeframe— think on the order of five decades or more—we are probably going to see effects due to sea level rise. Obviously, in addition to sea level rise potentially causing the migration of hundreds of millions of people, it would damage coastal infrastructure at a level worse than nuclear weapon use.

---

[144] For instance, there are some other gases (like methane) that are far more potent than carbon dioxide when it comes to the capacity to trap heat in the planet's atmosphere. Currently, these gases are not thought to influence global warming as much as carbon dioxide, as the quantity of carbon emissions is much greater than the other gases. However, this is assuming that potent feedback effects, involving things like methane hydrates, do not get activated as a result of the warmer temperatures and other associated changes.

However, despite the long-term nature of climate change, the next decade is probably the last opportunity to address the challenge effectively (partly because our energy supply, especially liquid fuels, may become too unpredictable after that time period). If we do not get our act together in that time frame, at least in terms of getting the next-generation energy source ready for deployment, and developing the requisite crop varieties, it is unlikely we will have the energy or resources to tackle the problem effectively later on.

2. UNRESOLVED TENSIONS (POTENTIAL FOR SYSTEM FAILURE)

Unlike the above discussions where mitigation response is a possibility, there are some areas where effective responses have not yet been identified. We may call these areas *unresolved tensions*. Some prominent unresolved tensions are mentioned in Table 13, and the practical consequence of a corresponding failure is noted alongside it. Fortunately, it remains possible that well-thought-out human actions can reduce the risks emanating from these tensions.

Table 13 Unresolved Tensions	
Potential Failures	Implication of Failure
Five Interconnected Tensions	
Not clear how to maintain high EROI in the system	Without it, nations may retreat to Stages II/III
No clear proposal has been presented for reforming the monetary system	An untethered monetary system increases the inequalities in wealth/income
Not enough fossil fuels for developing countries to become economically prosperous	Urgent need for new, high-EROI sources, so that the existing limits can be extended
Human impact on the planet's ecology has not yet stabilized	Loss of key species could lead to the collapse of parts of the food web
Not enough resilience to shocks coming from climate change	A potential collapse of states, if agriculture fails
Restraint-Function-Related Tensions	
Restraint-function's environmental responsibility	Lack of this responsibility may lead to collapse
Not clear how to eliminate nuclear weapons	Risk of some crisis remains

The seven tensions mentioned in Table 13 can be viewed as coming in two separate categories. This is because the last two tensions mostly hinge on our understanding of the Restraint-function, whereas the first five tensions do not deal with the Restraint-function directly.

A. EROI, Money, Resources, Species Loss, and Climate Change

The first five tensions can be summarized as follows: dropping EROI, unstable monetary system, energy and resource scarcity, species loss, and climate change. As we shall see in the discussion below, these five areas are tightly interconnected with one another.

Dropping EROI (Leads to a Disproportional Drop in Government's Ability)

In order to understand the impact from dropping EROI, it helps to view the impact in terms of declining *net energy* levels. Although the total energy supplies determine the country's GDP, it is the net energy level (energy available after the energy industry's requirements) that determines the country's prosperity level and its ability to collect taxes commensurate with the Stage-IV level.

This is because a large fraction of the total energy automatically gets used up in extracting, refining, and transporting fossil fuels, as well as the unavoidable supply chains associated with a renewable energy infrastructure. It is only the surplus or leftover energy (after the energy sector activities) that can be made available for use in the economy. When the EROI level declines, this leftover energy takes almost all the impact from the shrinkage (GDP need not shrink immediately), which disproportionally reduces the government's taxation and delivery capacity.

As a consequence, those nations that cannot maintain a high EROI may have no option but to retreat to a more primitive stage. Obviously, any retreat to earlier stages would be accompanied by loss of individual economic liberty, and perhaps even gross human rights violations. The solution to this tension cannot be modeled theoretically; it can only be solved by some scalable energy technology with a high EROI.

Unstable Monetary System

The second tension is that there is no specific proposal within the model on how to reform the monetary system. The current system is fatally flawed because it is a debt-based monetary system, which necessarily assumes perpetual exponential growth into the future. Anyone familiar with the mathematics of exponential functions knows that such a system will have to be periodically reset, lest it should crash under its own weight. After all, the resources available to us are not infinite. Not surprisingly, in the event of an overall EROI level that declines fast enough, such a reset becomes practically unavoidable.

To complicate the matter even more, the longer the current debt-based monetary system survives under its own steam, the worse the state of inequalities (in terms of wealth and income) will be within major countries like the US. This potentially creates an entirely separate pressure, one which might lead to unpredictable results at the political level. The solution to this tension will have to involve reforming the monetary system.

Energy and Resource Scarcity

The wealth inequality within nations created by the second tension can be viewed in a different way—in terms of the per capita energy availability (or resource availability) across nations. This alternate framing can be thought of as the third tension.

Based on the recent trends of economic growth, it seems as though the exponential growth in energy demand is destined to continue until people in most countries have access to an energy level that is roughly similar in per capita terms. In other words, things move till the average person in most countries has similar levels of wealth. Unfortunately, based on current patterns of resource usage, the situation envisioned above will place such an enormous demand on the planet's resources that it simply cannot be met by more fossil fuels.

Fortunately, there is sufficient solar insolation on the planet's surface that it appears even this high demand for energy can be met easily. Indeed, the cost of solar power has fallen dramatically to levels that make it competitive with fossil fuels. The key unknown here is whether the EROI of solar (or wind) power is high enough to allow a seamless transition from fossil fuels to solar power, especially when we consider the externalities that will enter the picture and reduce solar efficiencies. In particular, once solar power crosses key thresholds like 50 percent of the total grid power, there will be an enormous need for battery storage, which currently cannot be met.

If the solar EROI—when it is responsible for producing the majority of the grid power—is too low, then the current solar installations would be one-time installations made purely on the bounty supplied by the high EROI of present-day fossil fuels. Once the high EROI vanishes, the lower solar EROI may be hard-pressed to maintain the existing solar infrastructure. It probably cannot be maintained far beyond its designed life span of thirty to forty years (a steady deterioration in performance can be expected every year). Of course, the need to continue scaling up the infrastructure will be even harder to meet.

The danger is especially valid since the shale oil output (so far achieved only in the US) is vulnerable to rapid declines, at least much more so than the traditional oil fields.[145] Moreover, the EROI of shale oil may be a similar story as in the case of the externalities-laden solar power, since it cannot be relied upon to power modern civilization beyond a few short decades. Obviously, the only solution to this tension is that a new, scalable, high-EROI energy technology be developed and deployed on an immediate basis.

Species Loss and Climate Change

Both species loss and climate change are getting greatly accelerated due to human activities. When compared to the enormous species loss the planet is already experiencing, the planet's climate may seem more stable, at least from the short time frame of human life span. Unfortunately, that would be a wrong conclusion.

Given that the planet experienced an unusually moderate temperature range of about one degree centigrade for the last 10,000 years (compared to the far larger ten-degree centigrade changes seen often in the last 800,000 years), even some *mild* variation above one degree centigrade can easily cause the collapse of fragile artificial setups, like our elaborate agricultural system. If so, that could easily drop us back to a hunter-gatherer existence.

Thus, although humanity's harmful impact on species variety is serious, the second area of fossil fuel-induced climate change is even more serious. After all, the metric that matters is the effect on humans.[146]

---

[145] Coal and natural gas cannot replace the liquid fuels in the current energy matrix. First, liquid fuels cannot be replaced by non-liquid energy sources, at least not without a multi-decade effort in that direction. Second, climate change trends will be increasingly apparent in the future, making any attempt to increase the power supply from coal problematic. Although natural gas has lower levels of carbon emissions, it is likely to be accessible only if there is a pipeline for its transportation. Transporting Liquified Natural Gas (LNG) via ships comes at significantly higher costs than transporting a stable liquid fuel like oil.

[146] Admittedly, species loss definitely has the potential to become as serious as climate change if it reduces our ability to grow food (e.g., loss of bee species, etc.).

However, far from attempting to reduce the already apparent negative influence from the existing stock of fossil fuel emissions in the atmosphere, the global economy continues to increase its emissions.[147] Any serious break from the trend in the planet's climate will prove extremely difficult to correct, for science does not know how to *manage* the long-term future of a system that is as complex as the planet's climate.

There is no complete solution to this impact on climate. Even something as dramatic as stopping economic growth altogether will not suffice. It would still leave the historic greenhouse gas emissions in the atmosphere, where they would trigger an existential crisis for humanity. Besides, stopping economic growth surely cannot be considered while there are large inequalities in the wealth of people across the globe.

On the slightly brighter side, the two tensions posed by species extinctions and climate change can both be partly tackled by allocating a portion of the surplus energy (generated by a new, high-EROI system) to ecological restoration activity—especially activities like reforestation.

The Five Tensions Converge on Environmental Limits

Incidentally, the above five tensions can be understood in terms of the separate theses put forward by historians Joseph Tainter and Jared Diamond. While the first tension of dropping EROI roughly maps to Joseph Tainter's argument in his book *Collapse of Complex Societies* (it suggests that decreasing returns associated with increasing complexity in society eventually causes collapse), the next four tensions seem connected to two of the five factors mentioned in Jared Diamond's book

---

[147] It must be noted that with the consistent fall in the price of solar energy, it is becoming cheaper to resort to solar power than to coal. So, the trend of increasing emissions could soon change.

Collapse.[148] Notably, both Diamond's and Tainter's theses are built up from detailed observations of past civilizational collapses, rather than the strictly model-based approach that is taken in this work.

To sum up, the five tensions raise a virtual crying need to take up the *environmental limits* much more seriously. After all, the likely solutions to these tensions do not emerge directly from the Constitutional model (except perhaps the monetary system). Instead, they appear to require big technological and scientific breakthroughs.

However, if taken beyond the brink, species loss and climate change may not be solvable even with an infinite energy supply. Therefore, all things considered, the best that the model can do is to suggest some mechanisms within the Constitution, with a guarantee of funding, so that these areas can be addressed in a systematic manner.

B. Restraint-Function Related Tensions

Unlike the previous five tensions, which had complex inter-linkages with each other, the commonality between the last two tensions is simple—they are based on the presence of the Restraint-function.

Restraint-Function's Environmental Responsibility

Currently, Constitutions do not have any prominent function that explicitly bears the responsibility for mitigating environmental threats. In this

---

[148] The five factors identified by Diamond are environmental degradation, climate change, foreign trade, peace, and societal response. Incidentally, most of these factors are briefly mentioned in the first paragraph of Tainter's work as well. An example of environmental degradation is the phenomenon of ground level sinking in some large metropolises, like Mexico City and Jakarta. It is thought to be caused by an overexploitation of ground water. The situation in Jakarta is more problematic because it might experience encroachment from the sea.

connection, it is good that this model can provide for a Restraint-function whose responsibilities potentially extend directly to the environmental domain. If the Constitution gives it that responsibility, Restraint-function will have to make a scientific determination of the threats in the environmental domain and prepare a long-term action plan to mitigate the associated risks.

For instance, geophysical threats like tsunamis and earthquakes can be extremely devastating, but their frequency is unlikely to change due to human action. On the other hand, it is probable that an increase in extreme climatic events can be attributed to the existing stock of fossil fuel emissions present in the atmosphere. This means that while the latter (shocks from climate) must be actively reduced, the former (geophysical threats) can only be monitored for warning signs.

Needless to say, the part of the plan that attempts to reduce the detrimental human-influence on the environment will work only if there is active cooperation from Hohfeld's power-regulators. However, it may be surprising to learn that even the part of the plan for creating warning systems and high-EROI sources can proceed only under the ambit of power-regulators, like the head of government. That said, Restraint-function should be able to influence the head in the environmental area, as it is necessary to have Restraint-function's cooperation in many other matters if governance of the country is to be effective.

In other words, Restraint-function's job includes raising the profile of the environmental resilience plan, so that it gets at least the same priority as the country's defense forces.[149]

---

[149] This responsibility of Restraint-function was not explicitly mentioned earlier (it was lightly touched on in Table 12), since it might have appeared unnecessary when the potential costs of its non-implementation were still unclear to readers. It is better to talk about it in this chapter since we have clarified here that the system itself might fail due to environmental reasons.

Elimination of Nuclear Weapons

It is possible that the suggestion for a self-correcting system at the Intent Director level may become relevant at the Restraint-function's level as well. Obviously, while the self-correcting system at the Intent Director level would only need to hold within a country, the system at the Restraint-function level would have to hold internationally. But since there can be no centralized provisioning of justice at the international level, the success of a self-correcting system at the Restraint-function level is far less certain than at the level of Intent Directors.

Nevertheless, let us examine the benefits of such an international system. For starters, while this system can potentially enforce nuclear nonproliferation and perhaps even reduce nuclear weapons,[150] it may have other important benefits as well. For example, it can potentially reduce problems like the lack of rule-of-law in countries, environmental degradation, and perhaps even aggressive moves into problematic technologies by countries.

Admittedly, such a system would require a high level of maturity in the international community, in terms of advanced Constitutional arrangements in individual nation states, which unfortunately does not exist as yet.

As a result, a self-correcting ecosystem of Restraint-functions at the international level is probably too much to expect, at least as far as this generation is concerned. However, if we want to move toward an eventual elimination of nuclear weapons, and our short-term approaches toward

---

[150] Obviously, this does not seek to change any of the mechanisms regarding the current nuclear nonproliferation regime. This is only an attempt to add an additional layer of safety, which is certainly something we should work on. Similarly, Restraint-function's environmental responsibility would not seek to change any of the existing environmental agreements. It would look only to add an additional voluntary layer of safety.

that end prove unsuccessful, this seems like one of the more promising avenues that can be pursued.

Practical View on the Priority of Restraint-Function

Finally, in view of the last two discussions on the need for Restraint-function, it must be said that the bigger problem facing this generation is the facilitation of high-EROI energy sources and rule-of-law for commercial organizations, along with a concomitant undertaking to restore the planet's ecology. Perhaps it is only after those areas have been adequately addressed that we should look at other areas like the Restraint-function.

12

Avoidable
Misinterpretations

This final chapter on misinterpretations deals with the issues that come up as a result of the overall work. These areas have to be addressed separately here at the end, as it would have been difficult to include them in the earlier areas of the work.

Some remaining misinterpretations to be avoided are as follows:

1. Force-fitting the model as a top-down hierarchical system.
2. Force-fitting the model as biased toward a specific group.
3. Force-fitting Stage-III in the Rights model as giving priority to women over men.
4. Force-fitting the model to be the same as rights-based *Will* and *Interest* theories.
5. Force-fitting the model into a comparison with theories that are not rights-based.

6. Force-fitting the model as harming the long-term interests
   of some industries.

7. Force-fitting the Rights model as the main framework of
   human rights.

Attempting to Force-Fit the Model as
a Top-Down Hierarchical System

In the paradigm of human rights, everyone has equal rights and dignity. This is the core of the human rights view, and it cannot be changed. Therefore, as far as this model is concerned, the only acceptable situation is that people don't participate in any activity, unless it is of some voluntary interest to them.

For instance, at the level of the second row in Figure 3, people engage with others in the private space only if there is a mutual interest. Similarly, in the third row, people participate in public activities like voting only if it is of voluntary interest to them. Needless to say, at all levels higher than the above two, there is even less obligation on the individual to participate. This voluntary participation from the people can be understood as the working of bottom-up forces.

Moreover, the democratic feedback from people, which controls all Constitutional democracies, should not be viewed in terms of a top-down hierarchy. If one does argue for that position, it would essentially place all the citizens at the very top of the pyramid, which would be an absurd interpretation of *hierarchy*.

Keeping in mind the above two points about the voluntary participation of people and the democratic feedback from the people, it might be salutary to note that these two aspects are responsible for the delicate balancing act between the top-down (consolidating) forces and the bottom-up (morality) forces. Indeed, it is this balancing act that is visible in Figure 18.

Notably, as discussed in Figure 17a, there are at least two areas where discussion of top-down forces may not be out of place—taxation and dispute resolutions. However, it is the people's bottom-up need for security that creates the forces of taxation and the criminal justice system, both of which then get perceived as being top-down in nature, when they are looked at in isolation from the rest of the system.

In contrast to the mandatory nature of criminal dispute resolutions, the voluntary nature of Help-Right implies top-down forces have no access in the domain of civil disputes unless one party escalates the matter. One of the direct consequences of this situation is that something like a *uniform civil code* cannot be forced on citizens against their will. For instance, the Indian Constitution suggests that this is a worthy goal to aspire toward, but crucially, it does not make it mandatory. The structure of this model implies an enacted civil code cannot be made mandatory. It would become applicable only if the citizens voluntarily invoke it as the basis of their interactions with each other.

Attempting to Force-Fit the Model as
Biased toward a Specific Group

Any work seeking to be part of serious scholarly work cannot possibly seek to include all possible viewpoints within itself. If it attempts such a feat, it would lose its integrity and be filled with contradictions. Put another way, if it attempts to please everyone, it will find that task impossible. Consequently, there is little doubt that any direct attempt to appeal to diverse coalitions of people should be left to political practitioners. Incidentally, even politicians may not attempt to woo every group. Instead, they generally prefer to stop with those groups that provide them with the crucial advantage in elections.

The ability to serve all *individuals* equally, regardless of their ethnic, linguistic, and other preferences, arises not from the narrow considerations of politics, but from the rule-of-law within the Constitutional structure. Not only does this structure ensure all citizens are immune in the negative liberty space, but it also ensures that the country's positive liberty space serves all individuals equally, and this latter aspect sometimes even includes affirmative action in favor of disadvantaged sections. It is because both citizens and legal scholars continuously affirm this reality about the Constitutional structure that more aggressive factions within political parties cannot go overboard with their attempts at polarization.

In addition, it should also be pointed out that the quotes at the lower levels of the model are more important than those at the later higher levels. This is because of the non-adversarial imperative within the model. Since quotes at the lower levels are more important, it may be argued by some that the model favors those groups that are more aligned with those quotes. Obviously, since the model cannot exist without *all* its elements, this argument is completely devoid of merit. With regard to getting placed within the initial elements of the model, the world of ideas is an open forum where better ideas get ahead. Nothing stops people from coming up with better ideas, such that the existing quotes can be replaced with more complete views.

Attempting to Force-Fit Stage-III in the Model
as Giving Priority to Women over Men

There is probably a structural disadvantage for women in Stage-II systems across history, perhaps due to the natural attributes that evolution has bestowed on the human species. This is one of the main reasons why Stage-III is argued to be a better alternative. After all, the equal feedback inherent at the level of Stage-III would tend to redress this historical problem of gender disadvantage.

However, this problem of gender disparity at the Stage-II level certainly cannot be remedied by going to the opposite extreme and giving priority to women over men at the Stage-III level. The only feasible approach, and the only one that can be defended by the model, is to give all the people, regardless of their various attributes, equal say in how matters are conducted in the state.

In particular, it has become evident in recent times that the birth rates in developed countries have dropped far below the replacement rate of 2.1, partly due to the freedom justly won by women in those countries.[151] A notable outcome of this development is that unless some of these countries can get their fertility rate back up to the replacement level, they face a near existential crisis.[152]

Just as the model is in alignment with better girl-child education so as to reduce the birth rates in countries, it is also in alignment with tax

---

[151] Of course, it is now well-known that women's fertility rates decline when their education levels rise. For instance, the fertility rate is below the replacement rate even in Stage-II systems like that of China. It is also low in a theocratic country like Iran. However, the broader point about developed countries experiencing lower fertility rates is probably valid.

[152] If we assume the same conditions will hold in the future as well, and there is no reason why they would not, it is a mathematical certainty that the concerned countries cannot survive for long in their present situation (at least with respect to liberal measures like public welfare, etc.), unless the fertility rate is brought back up to 2.1.

and spending policies incentivizing more births in countries where birth rate has fallen below the replacement rate. Obviously, while countries can have overall goals, and perhaps some education and incentive policies for achieving those goals, it goes without saying that people's rights cannot be violated.

Moreover, the solution to this problem should not be to incentivize more births in such a manner that the state's taxes and spending are available disproportionally more to women than men. After all, such a situation would be tantamount to favoring women over men.[153] A possible implication of this stance is that if there are public policies aimed at raising the fertility rate back to the replacement rate, they ought to encourage two-parent households rather than single-parent households.[154] The basic caveat is that the Stage-III country's tax and spending policies should not end up giving disproportionate priority to women over men, once all the public policies are accounted for at the overall level.

Attempting to Force-Fit the Model to
Be the Same as Rights-Based Will
and Interest Theories

Since scholars have attempted to clarify the conceptual underpinnings of rights for some time now, there are several existing theories in this space.

---

[153] There can be public policies that prioritize a gender over another in some areas. For instance, women should receive better paid maternity leave options due to biological factors. Similarly, men are generally preferred in some arms of the defense forces and in several professions involving high physical stress. However, at the overall budget level, it is probably necessary to avoid bias for either gender.

[154] Perhaps an exception can be made to this possibility, in case there is a minority group that has a disproportionally high share of single-parent households, since their numbers could decline relative to the overall population. But even so, at the overall level, the policies must be designed to encourage two-parent households.

Perhaps the most prominent of these rights-based theories are the *Will* and *Interest* theories.

Basically, Will-theory of rights is premised on the idea that the right-holder is a voluntary agent. Since the Complementary Rights of the model are such that they can be thought of as *degrees of freedom* belonging to the individual, it may seem to agree with Will-theory. However, the model is also clear that some rights cannot be waived (e.g., immunity rights), which disagrees with Will-theory, since the latter considers all rights can be waived by the right-holder. Moreover, infants and comatose patients also have rights under the model, whereas they would not in Will-theory.

Meanwhile, according to Interest-theory of rights, the function of rights should be to further the right-holder's interests. In other words, it is not the choice made by the right-holder that is important, but whether those rights make the right-holder better off. Thus, this approach tries to create a listing of the necessary rights: welfare rights, healthcare rights, women's rights, and others. However, it may be impossible to create a comprehensive listing of rights by identifying the interests alone.

It may appear to a lay person that Interest-theory correlates with the claim and immunity part of the model, and Will-theory correlates with the privilege and power part of the model (refer to Figure 10). However, it is likely the two theories are more sophisticated in their approach than what such a simple characterization would seem to suggest. Essentially, this particular model cannot resolve the debate going on in the community regarding the nitty-gritty of various rights theories.

It was not made with that in mind. The model seeks only to map the working of Constitutional democracies in a reasonably accurate manner.

Attempting to Force-Fit the Model into
a Comparison with Theories That
Are Not Rights-Based

It is possible that there will be attempts to compare the model to theories on disparate topics, especially in the area of social sciences or humanities. This could include theories on economic ideologies (e.g., capitalism, socialism, etc.), ethical outlooks (e.g., Kant), or political party ideologies. Fortunately, since the model is explicitly meant for capturing a Constitutional structure that can enhance the rights framework, any proposed comparison to theories not fully committed to either Constitutional democracy or the human rights paradigm can be dismissed.

For instance, the model's coverage probably has some overlap with both capitalism and socialism, but these ideologies have too many wide-ranging connotations to be explicitly included within the model.[155] The core disagreement here might be about the validity of the fundamental principles. While this model considers human rights and Constitutional democracy as its core principles, economic ideologies will have a different set of privileged assumptions.

---

[155] For instance, both capitalism and socialism fail when taken to the extremes, as their underlying assumptions lack natural stability. Capitalism assumes the ability to grow the economy exponentially forever, which is not possible within a planet's finite ecology, and socialism assumes it is possible to focus on welfare alone, which is not possible without a productive private sector (the more extreme notion of public ownership of the means of production is not included in this model). Both of these approaches can work over short time frames when the resources are abundant. Obviously, capitalism takes longer to fail than socialism because the planet's resource base is much larger than can be provisioned by any private sector, but when the failure comes, it is likely to be more severe and perhaps even permanent. Clearly, if the approaches are to be truly sustainable over a longer time frame, they have to be pursued within the stable settings of something like the Constitutional model, which is something that most people of both positions would agree with. Notably, the model does include within it the core concepts of *private enterprise* and *public welfare*. In the former case, capitalism is moderated by the presence of other stakeholders, and in the latter case, the focus is on infrastructure projects.

However, while we should avoid comparison with economic ideologies, it may not be possible to avoid all comparison with Kant's ethics and
political party ideologies. After all, these two areas have connections to
rights and democracy, respectively.

As far as Kant is concerned, his idea that humans are to be treated as
ends in themselves and not merely means seems to imply the place given
to the root element in the model. However, if Kant's theory implies some
additional aspects as well, which do not seem immediately obvious from
the improvement-perspective discussed in Table 5.1, the model would have
to be considered as different from it. Nevertheless, the task of comparison
between the two theories must be mentioned because there may be some
overlap present between the model and Kant's analysis. For instance, the
terminology of *negative* and *positive* freedoms may have had their origin
in Kant's analysis.

Similarly, some may find it tempting to argue, perhaps based on Figure
19, that political party ideologies can be pigeonholed into one of the two
buckets of IP and GN liberties. This is clearly a mistaken approach and
has already been rebutted as part of the Figure 19 discussion, but perhaps
the point is important enough to be reiterated once more.

The mere existence of more than two political parties, which is the
norm in democracies, suggests that any attempt to pigeonhole political
party ideologies into occupying just one of the two democratic-input (i.e.,
GN and IP liberty) spaces is uncalled for. Instead, they should be thought
of as having the freedom to subscribe strongly to both democratic-input
liberties, since it is not advisable to leave vacant spaces in their appeal
to the voters. If a party defines itself as representing only one of the two
democratic-inputs, it is a sure road to failure. Active political ideologies
cannot be modeled from any limited set of assumptions. They depend

upon the regional context to a rather strong degree, mostly due to demographical, historical, and leadership factors.

Attempting to Force-Fit the Model as
Harming the Long-Term Interests
of Specific Industries

It may be argued by some that the model has the potential to hurt certain industries, especially in the short term. Of course, theoretically speaking, if something like a Constitutional model happens to criticize certain industries, it perhaps should not be considered a failure of the model. Indeed, in certain situations, it is the lack of criticism that should be seen as a failure.

However, from a more practical point of view, all tensions can introduce significant challenges in the short term, which makes it necessary that we address those concerns in a transparent and forthright manner. In this particular case, it may be argued that the adversely impacted list of industries includes the likes of fossil fuel companies, airlines, airports, large banks, and monopolies.

Regarding fossil fuel companies, both oil and natural gas have unique properties that make them indispensable for enabling the transition to the new energy paradigm, which should happen over the next three decades or so. However, the impact on coal will be unavoidable since that will be the first industry to be scaled down once an alternative energy source starts scaling up. Indeed, this impact has already started, due to the sharp drop in solar power prices. This probably cannot be helped, but governments can take extra interest in attracting other labor-intensive industries to the coal belts, so as to mitigate the impact on local jobs.

With regard to the air transport industry, the impact on airlines and airports from something like a carbon tax on international air passengers and cargo (perhaps domestic air traffic as well) will not be serious enough to challenge their business models, since the impact will be uniform across the whole industry. However, it is possible that some of their loans will need repackaging from the banks, which can be done, since the number of flights flown may not see much shrinkage.

On larger banks, it has been suggested that they should be broken up once they cross a certain size, perhaps with respect to the country's GDP. However, such a development does not harm any stakeholder in the long run. Rather, it creates more leadership roles for banking personnel to move into. It is also suggested that bank employee salaries should not be linked to the short-term profits of the banks.[156] This will reduce short-term profiteering by some banking personnel and will be of great benefit to all those bank employees who want to see their long-term service being rewarded.

On monopolies, organizations crossing a pre-agreed threshold of market power would be subjected to antitrust activities, such that they can no longer be thought of as being a monopoly. Therefore, monopolies are defined as only those organizations where the antitrust approach will not yield the desired results. There are some significant suggestions in the area of these *unavoidable monopolies*. Yet, none of the stakeholders in these monopolies lose out as a result of those suggestions, including even the shareholders. The suggestions have to be significant because without some major changes, everyone other than those shareholders who seek strictly short-term gains will lose out.

---

[156] Admittedly, this position about regulating higher salary levels in banks is likely to be unpopular (to put it mildly) among those banking personnel who draw especially high remunerations. Unfortunately, it is not possible to please everyone at the same time, at least not if the model is to be true to its goal of furthering individual freedom.

Finally, a simple, generic analysis can make it clear that the model will actually have a beneficial impact on all commercial sectors. The generic conclusion is essentially unavoidable if we prioritize the concept of market capitalization over the other metrics used in the marketplace. After all, market capitalization is the most encapsulating metric in capitalism. As market capitalization is entirely reducible to the present value of an organization's expected future profits, it stands to reason that in an unsustainable global economy, market capitalization will collapse due to the fall in the prospects of future profits. It is only in a sustainable global economy that the market can continue to justify an expectation with regard to future profits.

In other words, unless market capitalization is thought of as recording just the short-term profit possibility, which obviously can't be defended because that would be like defending Ponzi schemes, this model will help all commercial undertakings. Incidentally, this is also what the people want since they want to get their needs serviced in a better manner through entities competing among themselves for that role.

Attempting to Force-Fit This Model as the Main Framework of Human Rights

The fact that the model cannot be applied in all situations may be a fault, but it is not its biggest fault.[157] For instance, the focus of the model on improving liberty in the public space (and staying out of private spaces) may even be considered a good thing. The real problem with the model

---

[157] Some prominent situations where the model cannot be applied include the likes of Stage-II systems, Restraint-less systems, federal systems, etc.

is that the human domain must primarily be understood in terms of human values, and the model is mostly unsuitable for conveying that aspect. Admittedly, some effort has been made in this direction by using well-known quotes, but that alone cannot make up for the shortcoming.

Fortunately, a framework like UDHR does that job much better, perhaps because it makes no attempt to build a Constitutional structure. Besides, this model fails in the face of violence, but UDHR may be more resilient due to its recognition of the *last resort* option (mentioned in Chapter One). Therefore, there is little doubt that the *main* framework for Constitutional studies should be a document like UDHR, on which there is a wide international agreement.

Moreover, it has already been acknowledged in this work that this particular model may not be the best way to understand the Constitutional structure. There may be other logical structures which make even more sense. Also, although the model covers a lot of territory, it is rather fragile to changes in understanding with regard to its earliest elements, namely the root and the Golden Rules. Any changes in those areas could have a cascading impact with the potential to change the entire model. Of course, this is also true if there are changes in the understanding of the four sovereign-liberties, and indeed, such changes cannot be ruled out following scholarly reviews of this work.

There are also many areas where the model has the potential to fail completely, even if it is only because of the impact from unpredictable environmental threats. For instance, there is the need for security while engaging in trade on the high seas. It is not an exaggeration to say that no model—perhaps with the exception of UDHR—can be treated as practically relevant on its own, without an adequate system for maintaining the security apparatus ecessaryy for international trade. Indeed, if the international impact of the monetary system reform suggested in Chapter Nine has a potential to reduce that security, it should be rejected. The solution might be to compensate the high seas security providers, at least until the Restraint-functions of the various nations become sufficiently mature.

Some other ways in which the model can fail are examined in Chapter Eleven. Several of the unresolved tensions (though not all) are amenable to logical reasoning, like the domestic monetary system, high-EROI energy sources, and others. Therefore, it is quite possible that another model might come along, which does better job in these specific areas. For instance, domestic monetary systems can be addressed from the domain of economics, and high-EROI energy sources can be addressed from the domain of science and technology. Law is also important here because implementing high-EROI systems will require a concomitant reform of the organizational boards. Similarly, monetary system supervision will need legal backing.

All these areas are strong and vibrant enough that they are likely to produce altogether independent, logical models, which will limit the applicability of this particular model.[158] All of these minor models will have to be plugged into a larger, resilient UDHR-like human rights paradigm that will serve as the main framework.

---

[158] However, the ideals underpinning the model, that it is human liberty which has to be maximized in an environment of nonviolence, and that the paradigm of human rights is the best means for doing that, appear to be rather hard to improve.

Request for Feedback

If you liked this book, it would be great if you could show your appreciation by giving a review.

It is possible some ideas from readers might make its way into the later books. Although the second book in this three-part series will likely be finalized by the time this book is published, the third book has got some way to go. Besides, a combined edition of all three books is probably several years away, and that certainly gives time for evaluating new ideas and associated feedback.

Also, please consider discussing the central ideas of this book with your friends. It is quite possible such discussions might lead to new insights.

Glossary

1. **Constitutional structure**: Constitutional structure is thought to be the basic structural framework present in the figures and tables of this work.

2. **Constitutional model**: Constitutional model can be understood as the above-mentioned Constitutional structure along with all the explanatory text in the chapters.

3. **Complementary Rights**: These are the Rights (possessed by the individual) which add up to the Constitutional model.

4. **Non-adversarial imperative of the model**: Non-adversarial imperative of the model (or constitutional logic) asserts that Complementary Rights cannot contradict the earlier Complementary Rights in the model.

5. **Initial expansion of the model**: This refers to the first four Complementary Rights in the model. They are easily recognizable from the pattern of doubling they bring to the model. Although the fifth Right (i.e., Regulation-Right) also shows this doubling property, its defining characteristic of regulation is more closely associated with the later consolidation of the model.

6. **Later consolidation of the model**: Later consolidation of the model is represented by the four Complementary Rights that come after the initial expansion of the model but before the final Feedback-Right. It starts with the Regulation-Right and ends with the Enactment-Right. They look to regulate the functioning of the system.

7. **Negative rights**: Mandatory inaction of the state with respect to the citizens.

8. **Positive rights**: Mandatory action of the state with respect to the citizens.

9. **Empowered-regulators**: These are the regulators responsible for managing the public spaces created by the Sovereignty-Right. There are four of these at the sovereignty level and another four at the commercial level.

10. **Natural regulators**: These are regulatory spaces where government cannot interfere, because they are already effectively regulated by natural forces.

11. **Nonviolent democracy**: A democracy which has not only implemented the empowered-regulators, but has also achieved an effective self-correcting balance at the later consolidation level of the model.

12. **Developmental extension**: This refers to the extension of the model where the functioning of commercial organizations becomes mature.

13. **Organizational spaces**: Refers just to the commerce spaces in the model's developmental extension. This is where the features dealing with commercial organizations are enabled.

14. **Infra-organization**: Commercial organizations that volunteer to perform some government projects, perhaps on a contract basis.

15. **Power-regulators**: Regulators on the left-hand side of the model.

16. **Immunity-regulators**: Regulators on the right-hand side of the model.

CHAPTER TWO

1. **Evolutionary stages**: These are the distinct evolutionary stages embedded within the model, and which seem to be experienced by various real-world systems.

2. **Stage-I, Stage-II, Stage-III, and Stage-IV**: Stage-I refers to hunter-gatherer systems; Stage-II refers to systems with undemocratic authoritarian governments; Stage-III refers to democracies that have not yet achieved the prosperity of Stage-IV systems; and Stage-IV refers to democracies that have achieved sustainable economic prosperity.

3. **Evolutionary cul-de-sac**: Culs-de-sac are defined as societal bottlenecks that can thwart the evolutionary progress of systems. There are three culs-de-sac defined in the model with each being associated with Stage-II, Stage-III, and Stage-IV, respectively.

4. **Tyrannical-rule**: Stage-II cul-de-sac which prevents the achievement of Stage-II empowered-regulators.

5. **Majoritarian-rule**: Stage-III cul-de-sac which prevents the achievement of Stage-III overall-regulators.

6. **Corporate-rule**: Stage-IV cul-de-sac which prevents the achievement of Stage-IV developmental-regulators.

7. **Separation-of-powers**: This refers to the three distinct types of regulators associated with the Stage-II, Stage-III, and Stage-IV systems. These are the empowered-regulators, overall-regulators, and developmental-regulators.

8. **Empowered-regulators**: Defined above in Chapter One.

9. **Overall-regulators**: This refers to three regulators: Bicameral Legislature, Supreme Court, and the head of government. This is the closest analogue in the model to the traditional understanding of the three arms of government: Legislature, Judiciary, and Executive.

10. **Developmental-regulators**: Regulators necessary to achieve the sustainable economic prosperity of Stage-IV.

11. **Head of government**: It could either be the president or the prime minister, depending on the type of government that has been implemented.

12. **Rule-of-law**: This refers to the implementation of the model on its right-hand side. It is being hyphenated to distinguish it from the existing usage of the term *rule of law* since some may argue that the existing usage is not exactly the same.

13. **Rule-of-privacy**: Judiciary protects the private spaces of the people.

14. **Rule-of-transparency**: Control-function ensures that the conduct of public servants is justiciable.

CHAPTER THREE

1. **CHQ factors**: The three factors of public servants that are justiciable by the people, namely cost, honesty, and quality.

2. **Control-function**: Control-function is the regulator in charge of the CHQ factors of public servants, so as to ensure the rule-of-transparency.

3. **Table 4.1, Table 4.2**: These two tables list the details associated with the Control-function at the Stage-II level and the Stage-III level, respectively.

4. **Remaining Rights**: While the third chapter defines Remaining Rights as all Complementary Rights that come after the Sovereignty-Right, it may be more accurate to think of these as referring to all Complementary Rights that come after the Help-Right. The model almost exclusively looks at the space of these Remaining Rights rather than at the first two Rights.

CHAPTER FOUR

No new terms are introduced.

CHAPTER FIVE

1. **Working dynamics**: Internal workings of the model at the level of sovereignty and later at the levels of Stage-III and Stage-IV.

2. **Lower limits**: Minimum factors necessary for achieving stability at the level of sovereignty and later at the levels of Stage-III and Stage-IV.

3. **Negative liberty**: Isaiah Berlin defines it as, *"What is the area within which the subject—a person or group of persons—is or should be left to do or be what he is able to do or be, without interference by other persons?"*

4. **Positive liberty**: Isaiah Berlin defines it as, *"What, or who, is the source of control or interference that can determine someone to do, or be, this rather than that?"*

5. **Maintenance-perspective, Improvement-perspective**: If maintenance-perspective can be understood as the status quo take on freedom favored by

Berlin, improvement-perspective can be understood as the opposite perspective which favors an improvement of freedom.

6. **Statutory-position, Normative-position**: Statutory and normative positions (largely self-explanatory terms) are defined as the two complementary views that exist within the improvement-perspective, just as negative and positive liberties are the two complementary views that exist within the maintenance-perspective.

7. **Sovereign-liberties (IN, GN, IP, GP)**: The four sovereign-liberties of IN, GN, IP, and GP refer to Individual Negative liberty, Group Negative liberty, Individual Positive liberty, and Group Positive liberty. In the two negative liberty strands, the Individual and Group are the subjects enjoying their liberty. On the other hand, when it comes to positive liberty, they are the agents doing the action.

8. **Democratic-inputs**: This refers to the empowered-regulators on the left-hand side of the model (Legislature and Executive) and the adjacent functional spaces they are responsible for regulating (GN and IP liberty).

9. **Sovereignty-grid**: When the four sovereign-liberties are mapped onto a three-by-three grid, so that they are placed on the outer rows and columns, we get the sovereignty-grid. This is shown in Figure 16.

10. **Minimum liberty space, Bottom-up stability**: These are two mechanisms by which some of the minimum factors necessary for the stability implied by lower limits can be achieved. While minimum liberty space refers to the minimum level of functional activity (rule-of-law-related) that must be achieved by the system, bottom-up stability refers to the prerequisites that must be present.

CHAPTER SIX

1. **External-stability**: Refers to the stability of the system with respect to the outer environment. This is illustrated using Figure 18.

2. **Internal-stability**: Refers to the stability of the system with respect to its inner forces. This is illustrated using Figure 19.

3. **Restraint-function**: A function which can potentially bring stability to the system in the domain of external affairs.

4. **Environmental threats**: These are those threats which exist in the outer environment but are completely outside the traditional domain of foreign affairs.

5. **Upper limits**: This can perhaps be understood as the limits beyond which the functioning of the model will break down in unpredictable ways. Since the above definition is less than satisfactory, the concept is explained by referring to the lower limits that have already been discussed. Consequently, we use the two concepts of maximum liberty space and top-down stability to understand upper limits.

6. **Maximum liberty space, Top-down stability**: These are two mechanisms by which some of the stability that is associated with *upper limits* can be achieved. While *maximum liberty space* refers to the level beyond which a system will break down, in more practical terms, it refers to the functional activity (democratic-inputs-related) that is responsible for increasing the liberty of individuals in the system. Meanwhile, *top-down stability* refers to the need for *peace* in international affairs.

CHAPTER SEVEN

1. **Embedded-regulators:** Refers to the four regulators in the private organizational spaces. Since the private organizational space is an artificial construct, we refer to the regulators associated with them as embedded-regulators (and not as natural regulators).

2. **Table 4.3**: This table details the Control-function duties at the infrastructure level.

3. **UBI**: Universal Basic Income. It is a welfare proposal meant only for stable Stage-IV systems.

4. **ODSI**: Abbreviation of Owners, Discretion, Services, and Infrastructure. It is a framework for working the model purely from the perspective of the two democratic-inputs (GN and IP liberties).

5. **EROI**: Energy Return over Energy Invested. This metric is necessary to understand the superior capacity of Stage-IV systems.

CHAPTER EIGHT

No new terms are introduced.

CHAPTER NINE

1. **Monetary system**: The system of rules within a country which determines the characteristics of its money (means of exchange).

2. **Table 4.4**: This table details the Control-function duties at the Stage-IV level. It deals with the governance issues around banks and monopolies.

CHAPTERS TEN THROUGH TWELVE

No new terms are introduced.

Acknowledgments

I want to thank everyone who has directly or indirectly contributed toward making this project a success. This includes all my friends, family, colleagues, mentees, mentors, professors, and close acquaintances.

Notably, this work simply could not have been done without the internet. Although Wikipedia is the most prominent example of an online repository that influenced the writing of this book, it is certainly not the only one. Countless other websites also played a part. The people behind them deserve our thanks.

Also, a special thanks is owed to Scribe Media and their author-friendly publishing process. This book might have taken a few more years to be published without their ready engagement.

Bibliography

CHAPTER ONE

1. Ambedkar, B. R. (1936). *The Annihilation of Caste*. New Delhi: Arnold Publishers, 1970.

2. Arendt, H. (1969). *Reflections on Violence*. The New York Review of Books.

3. Bolivar, S. (1951). *Selected Writings of Bolivar [2 Vol. Set]: Vol. 1: 1810–1822; Vol. 2: 1823–1830*. Compiled by Vicente Lecuna. Translated by Lewis Bertrand. New York: The Colonial Press, Inc.

4. Bolivar, S. (2014). *Carta de Jamaica (Memoria) (Spanish Edition)*. Linkgua.

5. Burke, E. (1968). *Reflections on the Revolution in France*. Penguin Classics.

6. Confucius. (1993). *The Analects*. Translated by Raymond Dawson. Oxford World's Classics.

7. Confucius. (1979). *The Analects (Lun yu)*. Translated by D.C. Lau. Penguin Books.

8. Hayek, F. (1960). *The Constitution of Liberty*. University of Chicago Press.

9. Hippocrates. (1923). *Hippocrates Collected Works I*, Edited by W. H. S. Jones (trans.). Cambridge: Harvard University Press.

10. Hohfeld, W. (1913). *Some Fundamental Legal Conceptions as Applied in Judicial Reasoning*. 23 Yale Law Journal.

11. Madison, J., Hamilton, A. and Jay, J. (1982). *The Federalist Papers*. Bantam Classics.

12. Mandela, N. (1995). *Long Walk to Freedom*. Back Bay Books.

13. Mencius. (2005). *Mencius*. Translated by D.C. Lau. Penguin Classics.

14. Nariman, F. (2013). *The State of the Nation*. Hay House Publishers.

15. Nkrumah, K. (1957). *Ghana: The Autobiography of Kwame Nkrumah*. Thomas Nelson & Sons.

16. Rand, A. (1943). *The Fountainhead*. The Bobbs-Merrill Company.

17. Roosevelt, E. (1960). *You Learn by Living*. Harper & Row, Publishers, Inc.

18. Smith, A. (2003). *The Wealth of Nations*. Bantam Classics Edition.

19. Stetson, C. (2007). *Creating the Better Hour: Lessons from William Wilberforce*. Stroud & Hall.

20. Teachout, Z. (2016). *Corruption in America: From Benjamin Franklin's Snuff Box to Citizens United*. Harvard University Press.

21. United Nations. "Universal Declaration of Human Rights." www.un.org/en/universal-declaration-human-rights/. (Last accessed on May 3, 2022).

CHAPTER TWO

1. Acemoglu, D. and Robinson, J. (2013). *Why Nations Fail: The Origins of Power, Prosperity and Poverty*. Profile Books.

2. Montesquieu, C. (2011). *The Spirit of the Laws*. Translated by Thomas Nugent. Cosimo Classics.

3. Nightingale, F. (2015). *Notes on Hospitals*. Dover Publications.

CHAPTER THREE

1. Cullison, A. (1967). *A Review of Hohfeld's Fundamental Legal Concepts*. 16 Cleveland. Marshall Law Review. 559.

2. Hart, H. (1982). *Essays on Bentham: Studies in Jurisprudence and Political Theory*. Oxford: Clarendon Press.

3. Hohfeld, W. (1917). *Fundamental Legal Conceptions as Applied in Judicial Reasoning*. 26 Yale Law Journal.

4. Lyons, D. (1970). *The Correlativity of Rights and Duties*. Nous. 4:45–57.

5. MacCormick, N. (1982). *Legal Right and Social Democracy*. Oxford: Oxford University Press.

6. Nightingale, F. (2012). *Notes on Nursing: What it is and what it is not*. Tredition Classics.

7. Saunders, K. (1990). *A Formal Analysis of Hohfeldian Relations*. 23 Akron L. Rev. 465.

8. Shue, H. (1996). *Basic Rights: Subsistence, Affluence, and US Foreign Policy*. Princeton: Princeton University Press.

9. Wellman, C. (1995). *Real Rights*. Oxford: Oxford University Press.

10. Wenar, L. (2021). "*Rights*." The Stanford Encyclopaedia of Philosophy (Spring 2021 Edition). Edward N. Zelta (ed.), https://plato.stanford.edu/archives/spr2021/entries/rights/ (Last accessed on May 3, 2022).

11. Wikipedia. "Human rights." https://en.wikipedia.org/wiki/Human-rights (Last accessed on May 3, 2022).

12. Wikipedia. "Rights." https://en.wikipedia.org/wiki/Rights (Last accessed on May 3, 2022).

CHAPTER FOUR

1. Catton, W. (1982). *Overshoot: The Ecological Basis for Revolutionary Change*. University of Illinois Press.

2. Hinton, D. (2013). *The Four Chinese Classics: Tao Te Ching, Chuang Tzu, Analects, Mencius*. Counterpoint.

3. Meadows, D. (2004). *Limits to Growth: The 30-Year Update*. Chelsea Green Publishing.

4. Mencius. (2011). *The Works of Mencius*. Translated by James Legge. Dover Publications.

CHAPTER FIVE

1. Berlin, I. (1969). "Two Concepts of Liberty" in *Four Essays on Liberty*. Oxford University Press.

2. Donnelly, J. (2013). *Universal Human Rights in Theory and Practice*. Cornell University Press.

3. Holmes, S. and Sunstein, S. (1999). *The Costs of Rights*. New York: W. W. Norton.

4. Kant, I. (2002). *Three Critiques, 3-volume Set: Vol. 1: Critique of Pure Reason; Vol. 2: Critique of Practical Reason; Vol. 3: Critique of Judgment*. Hackett Classics.

5. Stewart, D. (1829). *The Works of Dugald Stewart: Account of the Life and Writings of Adam Smith, LL.D.* Cambridge: Hilliard & Brown.

CHAPTER SIX

1. Austin, G. (1972). *The Indian Constitution: Cornerstone of a Nation*. Oxford University Press.

2. Austin, G. (2003). *Working in a Democratic Constitution: A History of the Indian Experience*. Oxford University Press.

3. Zeihan, P. (2016). *The Accidental Superpower: The Next Generation of American Preeminence and the Coming Global Disorder*. Twelve.

CHAPTER SEVEN

1. Hall, C. (2017). *Energy Return on Investment: A Unifying Principle for Biology, Economics, and Sustainability*. Springer.

2. Hall, C. and Klitgaard, K. (2012). *Energy and the Wealth of Nations: Understanding the Biophysical Economy*. Springer.

3. Hall, C., Balogh, S. and Murphy, D. (2009). *What is the Minimum EROI that a Sustainable Society Must Have?* Energies 2009, 2, 25–47; doi: 10.3390/en20100025.

4. Martenson, C. (2011). *The Crash Course: The Unsustainable Future of Our Economy, Energy, and Environment*. Wiley.

5. Professor Bartlett's Lecture on *Arithmetic, Population and Energy*: https://youtube.com/watch?v=F-QA2rkpBSY (Last accessed on May 3, 2022).

CHAPTER EIGHT

1. Bartlett, A. (2004). *The Essential Exponential! (For Future of Our Planet)*. University of Nebraska Lincoln.

2. Bricker, D. and Ibbitson, J. (2019). *Empty Planet: The Shock of Global Population Decline*. Constable & Robinson.

3. Hayek, F. (1991). *The Fatal Conceit: The Errors of Socialism*. University of Chicago Press.

4. West, G. (2017). *Scale: The Universal Laws of Growth, Innovation and Sustainability in Organisms, Economies, Cities and Companies*. W&N.

CHAPTER NINE

1. Booth, D. (2017). *Fed Up: An Insider's Take on Why the Federal Reserve is Bad for America*. Portfolio.

2. Prins, N. (2018). *Collusion: How Central Bankers Rigged the World*. Nation Books.

3. Piketty, T. (2017). *Capital in the Twenty-First Century*. Harvard University Press.

4. Reich, R. (2020). *The System: Who Rigged It, How We Fix It*. Knopf.

5. Reinhart, C. and Rogoff, K. (2009). *This Time is Different: Eight Centuries of Financial Folly*. Princeton University Press.

CHAPTER TEN

1. Rutherford, A., Lupu, Y., et al. (2018). *Inferring Mechanisms for Global Constitutional Progress*. Nature Human Behavior 2. Pages 592–599.

2. Tepper, J. and Hearn, D. (2018). *The Myth of Capitalism: Monopolies and the Death of Competition*. Wiley.

CHAPTER ELEVEN

1. Bastin, J., Finegold, Y., et al. (2019). *The Global Tree Restoration Potential*. Science. Vol. 365, Issue 6448, pp. 76–79. https://science.sciencemag.org/content/365/6448/76 (Last accessed on May 3, 2022).

2. Bock, L. and Burkhardt, U. (2019). *Contrail Cirrus Radiative Forcing for Future Air Traffic*. Atmospheric Chemistry and Physics. 19, 8163–8174, 2019.

3. Diamond, J. (2013). *Collapse: How Societies Choose to Fail or Succeed*. Penguin UK.

4. Hawken, P. (ed.) (2017). *Drawdown: The Most Comprehensive Plan Ever Proposed to Reverse Global Warming*. Penguin Books.

5. Le Page, M. (2019). *It Turns Out Planes Are Even Worse for the Climate than We Thought*. New Scientist. https://www.newscientist.com/article/2207886-it-turns-out-planes-are-even-worse-for-the-climate-than-we-thought/ (Last accessed on May 3, 2022).

6. Lewis, S., Wheeler, C., et al. (2019). *Restoring Natural Forests Is the Best Way to Remove Atmospheric Carbon*. Nature 568, 25–28. https://www.nature.com/articles/d41586-019-01026-8 (Last accessed on May 3, 2022).

7. Tainter, J. (1990). *The Collapse of Complex Societies*. Cambridge University Press.

8. Wikipedia. "Global temperature record." https://en.wikipedia.org/wiki/Global_temperature_record (Last accessed on May 3, 2022).

CHAPTER TWELVE

1. Kramer, M., Simmonds, N., and Steiner, H. (1998). *A Debate Over Rights*. Oxford: Oxford University Press.

2. Raz, J. (1986). *The Morality of Freedom*. Oxford: Oxford University Press.